The Day Hospital
a memoir

by ▮▮▮▮ ▮▮▮▮

For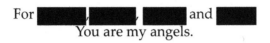
You are my angels.

Contents

Preface

This book tells very personal details of my life that I have shared with very few people. I wrote it in a burst of energy and optimism. I had recently risen, not unlike a phoenix, from a deep and lasting depression. In this state of newfound enthusiasm and purpose, I was feeling very open. I didn't want any more secrets. I no longer wanted to hide the shame of my story. I believe in busting the stigma of mental illness. I admire people who have been vulnerable with details of their own recovery journey. I want to be that real, because according to Brené Brown, vulnerability begets connection. I want more connection in my life. I put my name on the front of this book and was ready to share it with the world.

Thankfully I have solid, grounded people in my life who see the bigger picture. I was encouraged by several friends and family members who read early drafts to write this book under a pseudonym. They advised that my identity needs to be protected from being linked to these stories. This book is raw, revealing more personal health information than my medical records. But making up a fake name also feels a bit silly. This story is mine.

I have vacillated about whether or not to put my name on it, haters be damned. But in our online world today, stories get twisted and truth is amorphous. I don't want an out-of-context diagnosis to follow me for the rest of my career, let alone the rest of my life. I have mouths to feed. I am on a leadership track in a large professional organization. As much as they trumpet their passion for addressing mental health issues, I'm not sure if my career will continue to progress in an upward trajectory with this diagnosis linked to my name. Would a hiring manager google me and find words that would scare them off, no matter how sparkling my resume and reputation? Hiding from stigma is about surviving in an unforgiving world.

I'm not ashamed of these experiences. I used to be. I hope to reveal my name on the cover of a later edition of this book, maybe when I retire and have no more fucks to give. Instead of changing a lot of details including my name and all of the others in this book to pseudonyms, I decided to black them out. This may be jarring to the flow, my editor warned me, but I want it to be. I want it to be a reminder of the stigma that keeps me and so many others in the dark every single day of our lives. Mental illness is jarring. It never shows up at a convenient time.

Some pages of this manuscript resemble a redacted report coming out of the halls of government. Sorry, but you don't have top secret security clearance. If I have personally given you a copy of this myself, consider the clearance granted… you know who I am… go ahead and fill in all the names that I blacked out. For everyone else, I invite you to insert the names of people you know who have struggled with mental illness. Insert your name where mine is hidden, or where I have blacked out the names of those who supported me. Mental health is not an individual story—it affects everyone in the orbit of the person struggling. We all struggle.

This story is universal. These stories are not just about me, ████ ██████—they are about you. Thank you for indulging my need to protect my privacy and the privacy of my family. Besides my name, I have held little else back. This book is for you and the people in your life with stories like this to tell. Own your story.

March 2020

The Day Hospital
a memoir

by

1

The Day Hospital

It is raining. In the Pacific Northwest. In November. Big surprise. Good thing I have a nice raincoat and sturdy shoes. I shower and shave and kiss my wife goodbye and drop my daughter off at school. Just like any other day in 2019. But today I skip the exit to my office, nodding as I drive past the skyscraper that I spend most weekdays in. My route takes me east, over a long bridge and away from the city. Soon I am driving down a wide boulevard of brilliantly fall-hued trees. I take another left into a low-slung office park, unassumingly nestled into the edge of this suburban city. I pull into the parking lot, kill the engine and the radio, and take a deep breath. I have been here before, but only once last week, and never alone. A sign, just large enough to read from a distance, states "Psychiatric Day Hospital" with an arrow to the left and "outpatient clinic" to the right.

The actual hospital, the one with the ER and the surgeons and the big medical equipment, is down the road a mile. The day hospital is somewhere in between. A hospital without beds. They feed you hospital food but you go home and sleep in your own bed. You can't leave until they discharge you, but you can stop showing up. Today I am checking in, facing my fears, getting help, and accepting that I can't do it on my own. It is one of the hardest, most humbling, days of my life.

How did I get here? **Boldfaced**, projected, are the things that I want people to see, that I am fine with them knowing. These, in **bold**, are the ones I want you to look at first; if I really trust you you might get bits and pieces of the rest. Less bold are the fears I share only with a select few. **I have an adult life. I have two children that are old enough to talk back. I pick up my kids on time from a daycare whose high tuition I can** barely **afford.** I am really stressed about money. **I have had a vasectomy. I listen to more classic nursery rhymes than the top 40. I have mastered the art of hand-to-hand combat that is buckling a screaming child into a carseat.** I don't sleep well. I can't remember the last time I woke up feeling rested. I'm struggling to make time for myself. **I've been married over a decade.** I don't remember the last time I took her out on a date. **I have a cubicle and business cards and regular meetings with the C-Suite of companies with revenues in the billions. I get my dress shirts pressed at the dry cleaners. I own several pairs of dress shoes** (that need polishing) **and more than one suit jacket. I like my co-workers and they like me,** but now that I have made it, I am afraid of what will happen if they learn my true colors. **I was recently interviewed as an expert on the morning news and have been featured on a number of podcasts, and just taught a workshop for a national organization and was paid for it. I am a sought-after speaker.** I feel like a fraud, I can fake it for awhile and no one has noticed yet. I don't have time to go to Toastmasters, the place that it's ok to admit how awkward I really feel. I have student loans in the **six figures,** but so **is my annual income. I talk to my accountant several times a year. I have a plan. I am on the verge of getting ahead, maybe even buying a house in a few years in this expensive city. My social**

media accounts all report a thoroughly happy and successful version of me. My life is full of struggle and contradiction but I keep moving. Always keep moving. **I am a fucking adult.** But I am not ok.

This isn't supposed to be happening to me. This was not in my official calendar. I have goals. I am going places. But today I am here. At the day hospital. This is the only place I am going. This is the new plan. All other plans were put on pause when depression brought me to my knees once again. I am having a breakdown.

I step out of the car and lock it with a "beep." I glance around the parking lot, making certain that no one sees which door I walk into. The parking lot was deserted as I strode across it. No one seems to care what I am up to, I guess. I open the door marked "Day Hospital."

"Ok," I say to myself, take another deep breath and step over the threshold and into the building. I walk towards the sign that says "check-in."

A passage from Carrie Fisher's brilliant memoir, *Wishful Drinking*, trotted through my mind as I walked toward the day hospital that morning. "Bipolar disorder isn't for sissies." I picture her reading from it with a martini glass in her hand, words slightly slurring, and a sly smile on her face. They say she is dead, but I saw her in the Star Wars movie over the holidays, so I'm not entirely convinced. As a bumper sticker said in my old stomping grounds, "I saw Elvis at Island Recycling." Maybe she's up there with the king sipping the last drops and breaking the bottles that my old neighbors threw out.

This story isn't about Princess Leia and the King of Rock and Roll...though it is as timeless as they are. It is a story of struggle and humanity and making a life when your brain isn't quite mainstream. "Bipolar disorder isn't for sissies" rattles through my brain with the raspiest of whispers that only Carrie Fisher can conjure. The statement brings a chuckle and wry smile when you hear it - short and sweet and so true. But it is also a gut punch, a reminder of heart-wrenching struggle. Of my cousin's suicide, of my estranged father's violence, of my brother's drug abuse and psychosis and incarcerations, my grandmother's unrelenting melancholy, and my own dark depressions.

It isn't just the illness that is hard... it's the stigma, the medication side effects, the hiding, the shame, the grieving of a healthy self lost or maybe stolen, and the loss of self-respect that if only you were stronger you could beat this, that you could be normal, be free. The ball and chain of serious mental illness is a life sentence. I am coming to realize, however, that it doesn't have to lock me out of a full and healthy life where goals and dreams are realized and people I love are all around. As the latest depression recedes, that is what I will tell myself anyway. Today I am buoyed closer to shore, after months and months of struggle in deep dark water. I reached out for help and was pulled up into this boat named the *Day Hospital*. The storm isn't over but I'll be safe here for awhile.

Sometimes passion and purpose can push us too far and we miss the sign that says, "great job, take a breather." After years working to get ahead I had finally found work that paid me well and was in line with my skills and passions, I have two kids, a lovely wife with an intense job of her own, and a lot of expenses. Depression started grinding me down, a slow rub at first but then, right when I thought I was rock solid, I woke up and realized that I was ground down below my threshold of stability.

I started taking more medication and going to counseling and trying to make my relationships work, but I was drowning and exhausted and more and more hopeless. I stopped into my office to pick something up one weekend and sat at my desk. Looking at my degrees and certificates of appreciation, articles about the programs I had built, professional licenses, pictures of my children, gifts from people I had managed and plaques from boards I had served on - the life that I had built, the accomplishments that I had made since I threw away the noose I had once tied for myself — it all felt so empty. I had a good life but I didn't feel good. I was just as lost and wretched as I had ever been.

Phone a friend

I glanced at my phone and decided to call a friend. It rang for what felt like an eternity but then he answered. ▮▮▮▮ is one of those friends that I've known so long that I don't ever have to explain anything and we can hang out without talking, or talk for hours, and it is just comfortable. I feel safe when he's around. He's a veteran and has had his own struggles since returning from Iraq, and we've bonded over hundreds of miles of biking in recent years. I didn't know what to say. I started by saying I was at work and talking about that — always a good topic for me to avoid what is really going on. And then I started to sob. Now I am all about crying in therapy or occasionally with my wife, but it doesn't seem to really happen much with my buddies—not that we are super macho and against it—it just doesn't really happen. So this felt like a big deal. I was a sobbing, slobbery mess. I'm glad that I did. I couldn't pretend I was ok anymore. It was like just after that moment of terror when you turn your back for a moment and lose your child in the grocery store. The kid is lost and you are freaking out, totally losing your shit. Deer in headlights. But then the kid comes tearing around the corner with a bag full of candy to show you. You still feel like a terrible person, but at least you have a cute friend to eat candy with now. He talked me down. "One step at a time," he said. I ate some candy that I had hidden in my desk. I took a deep breath and looked out the window.

My friend helped me make a plan for the rest of the day. I felt a little better, relieved, in this moment anyway, to no longer be a lost child with no one to look after him. I had a friend. I went home and had dinner with my family and watched TV until I fell asleep.

I tried to pull it together the next week and found myself barely getting through the days without breaking down. It was exhausting. I was barely able to keep faking it. I didn't care anymore. I tell myself that no one noticed (except for home—it took a noticeable toll at home), but that I had managed the optics at work very well. My projects were all on track, due in many ways to the multiple strong collaborators I had working with me. No one was shooting any concerned looks in my direction. I am probably wrong about that. If I was that good of an actor I would have a pool in my backyard.

One day I worked from home, but I couldn't work. I knew I couldn't in good conscience do any good for anyone. I cancelled all my meetings. I said I was "sick." I got back in bed. My mind opened the black closet of desperate methods and I was sorting through my options.

I wasn't meant for the world. "I can't do it, I'm sorry" kept running through my mind. My wife texted to check on how my day was going, as she often does. She didn't get a response so she called me. I was quiet and she could tell something was off as soon as I answered with a gravelly "hey." Finally I said "I can't do it, I'm sorry." She offered to come home and I didn't talk her out of it. There was urgency in her voice now. My voice was flat and muffled. I promised her I would stay in bed and not do anything else until she arrived. That was fine with me. I stared at the ceiling wanting to die, wishing I would have a heart attack and she would find me and everyone would celebrate my life and no one would ever know how weak I really am.

She soon arrived, fiercely beautiful as always, looking sharp in her professional blazer. Her piercing gray eyes sized me up and softened with concern. I continue to be amazed that this amazing woman has stuck with me this long. She knew when she walked in the room what I had heard her fearing on the phone. What she had quietly been observing for weeks and months as I had slowly deteriorated while trying to keep calm and carry on. What neither of us wanted to admit.

The black dog of depression was back and he wasn't going

away. She was there when this had been much worse, much darker. 14 years ago she had held my hand after my suicide attempt and never stopped holding it. She knew what she was getting into, that this desperate broken man was always just under the surface, but I'm not sure she really knew how hard it would be. But today we were in it together as we always had been.

I was far from the ledge, but for me, to twist that tired-out metaphor about diabetes and mental illness… suicidal thoughts for me are like insulin spikes for a brittle diabetic. It's one thing to have thoughts and have never ever acted on them. But I had acted on them, several times, even if many many years ago. That was a ledge I had promised myself I would never get so close to again.

She urged me to call my psychiatrist. I set an appointment for the next day, and after ensuring that I was safe he gave me the name of a day hospital treatment program he used to work at. He thought I would do well there. He agreed that if I got accepted that he'd sign off on some leave from work to complete the program. Another door. I closed the black door and called the day hospital. They scheduled an intake and held me a spot in the program. A new plan.

They were nice on the phone. I could come home for the night and still take my daughter to school in the morning. It was a plan I could live with. It was a plan I hated but I knew I had no choice. It was the off-ramp I needed.

The scariest part was talking to my boss. I planned to tell him after I was accepted into the program and had my doctor sign the FMLA paperwork, but he was alerted by HR that I had requested a 2-week leave. He texted me to check in about the request, to make sure I was ok, and I decided to bite the bullet and tell him what was going on. HR said I didn't have to, but I felt compelled to. He has been a strong advocate for mental health in our organization, so it felt like he wouldn't judge me, but he was also my boss. I was a rising star at work and he was my champion and my mentor. Would this admission lead to questions about my competence, my resilience, my ability to take on tough challenges and see them through? Would the promotions end? The conversation was short, and he was very supportive to say the least.

I was going to work for another day to button some things up and then I was off for two weeks to focus on my mental health. This was decidedly not a vacation. I was not happy, but definitely relieved. I couldn't really see beyond next week, but at least I could see beyond tomorrow. Relief, I'm discovering as an adult, is one of my favorite emotions—especially being a parent. We have so many occasions to worry, and most of the time, after the pressure of all the bad things that could have happened builds up, they vanish and relief fills the vacuum, floating and singing "everything's going to be alright." I wasn't all puffy clouds and rainbows, but I accepted that I was going to take a break and be open to the possibilities of recovery.

Intake

My wife drove me to the intake appointment with the psychiatrist at the day hospital. It was to decide if they were truly going to admit me to the program. I distinctly remember struggling to get dressed that morning. What do you wear to interview to be a patient at a mental hospital? I settled on my standard clean cut look, but not over- or under-dressed. I pulled on a V-neck sweater and khaki pants with slip on black leather shoes. I shaved. I put light pomade in my short hair. My "normal guy" look. I was a bit nervous: would I not be crazy enough for them to take me, or alternately, would I be too crazy and they'd send me off to the hospital in a straight jacket? Did I jump the gun on telling work I needed to be off for two weeks to go into a program? My mind went around and around.

The psychiatrist turned out to be a very nice Japanese man of small stature with soft piercing eyes and a dark purple sweater vest over his blue striped shirt. I handed him the leave paperwork that HR had emailed me. The office was sparse, clearly not where he spent most of his time. He fiddled with the computer, but soon found his place on the screen and started to type. His eyes mostly stayed on me as we talked, but he would intermittently look back at the screen that was prompting some of the questions. He asked me how I was feeling now, what medications I was on, what I had taken in the past, about my family history of mental illness, and the details of my symptoms in recent weeks. This part was all rather dry, and a story I had shared enough times it felt rehearsed—no longer raw, except lately.

I was subdued…a bit slumped in the chair. Still ever the actor, trying to decide what crazy, but not too crazy, actually looks like. It was exhausting and I was glad when it was over. Near the end, though, he scooted away from the computer and started scribbling diagrams on a piece of paper. He explained the way my medications work for my diagnosis in a way that I had never heard before. He explained why the depression kept coming back. He drew a squiggly line under a straight line, with a few deep valleys and some small hills above the line. The deep valleys represented the severe major depressions while the smaller dips represented the more minor episodes. Above the line was the hypomania—not as frequent as the depression, but still part of the cycle. I nodded in recognition. I knew this cycle well.

As we got up to leave he said I could check in with the front desk and a counselor would meet with me to talk more about the program. I thought he was going to say more but he didn't. As he started to open the door I said, "So do you think I can come to the program?" He seemed surprised by the question. "Oh yes," he said, "we can help you—we just needed to be sure you didn't need to go to inpatient hospital." I breathed a sigh of relief. He continued, "I will complete this leave paperwork and give it to the front desk for you." It turned out I was just the right amount of crazy.

I found my wife sitting near the window of the quiet lobby (no classical music here), a magazine on her lap but tapping a message out on her phone. Ever the multi-tasker…I would have floated away years ago were it not for her grounded, organized, steadfast attention to keeping our life together and on track. "How was it?" she says in an almost-whisper. "Fine," I say with a sigh, and slump down in the chair next to her. She takes my hand and rests it on my knee, our rings rubbing together. "Someone else… one of the counselors is going to come get me to talk more," I whisper. "Ok, good," she says. She can tell I don't feel like talking…my gaze glancing between the magazines on the coffee table and the fall leaves out the window. She goes back to scrolling and tapping on her phone. I feel my phone in my pocket, the ever-present promise of distraction, but I resist the temptation and look around the lobby, soaking in my surroundings. I have been so all over the place for so long, so scattered and distracted—right now I just want to be here. If this sterile clinical building is to be my salvation, I want to be aware of what I am getting into.

"██████?" I hear from across the lobby. A woman with straight blonde hair looks in my direction. She's professionally dressed and the type of woman I imagine I'd pursue if I was single—pretty in a secretly nerdy sort of way. She's holding a blue folder and walks slightly ahead of me down the hall. She looks back warmly and says, "Do you go by ████ or ████?" I mumble… "████ is fine." The ice is broken as she leads me into a conference room.

I have been in a lot of hospitals and therapists' offices and office buildings, and a lot of conference rooms. This was definitely a conference room. In an office park. It didn't feel like a hospital, despite the signs saying "day hospital" outside the front doors and all around the building. I was calm, dejected, accepting that this was happening. I was done acting. She seemed nervous—not sure whether it was the cadence of her voice or the intermittent eye contact that gave me that impression. Maybe she knew I worked in the field and had a feeling I would be more critical of how she did this intake with me. I had left that mask at home. I was here to be a patient, nothing more.

She asked me some of the same questions as the psychiatrist— what brought me here, how I had been feeling in recent weeks, what I hoped to get out of the program. We settled on some goals that she promised to write up and give me on the first day of the program. I think we talked for almost an hour, but I'm not sure what it was about. It is a blur. I was concerned about the other participants—would I be the craziest one? Or maybe I would seem normal and they were totally off their rockers? She assured me that it was other professionals like me, that they had had attorneys, physicians, technology managers, and many other types of people just like me. Like me. Privileged, with good private health insurance, not homeless, not battling the external demons of an unforgiving world, only buckling against the pressures of a privileged one, and whatever inner demons that helped deliver us there.

It seemed ok. I liked conference rooms. I liked her. She was warm and kind and smart. She listened well and reflected back the essence of what I said—what I meant—leaving out the noise of my extraneous rambles. The doctor was a little odd, but seemed caring and competent and had already taught me some new things about my illness. I was escorted back to the lobby with instructions to arrive promptly at 8:15 on Monday morning to check in. There would be more paperwork, and the first group would start at 8:30.

Day Hospital

We only had one car, and as the day hospital was far away from our usual combined route, we decided to rent another. I reserved a "Rav4 or similar," which is what we drove then to fit all of our stuff and carseats and groceries and selves. Now we would have two for the next two weeks.

"Or similar" turned out to be a 4X4 Jeep. I'm not a very macho guy, like at all, so it was funny to me to drive off in this alpha vehicle that looked more ready for the battlefield than my planned trips to the paved suburbs. But, there is still testosterone and a teenage boy inside of me and I couldn't resist gunning the engine as I pulled onto the freeway. I could definitely appreciate the powerful V6 that comes standard in a man-mobile like this. Vroooom! It brought a smile to my face. Maybe my mojo was still in there after all.

I arrived early the first day and was the first one in the conference room. They gave me a small notebook to collect handouts and notes. I made some Earl Grey tea. After what felt like an eternity someone else came in. I figured them for another patient. They looked normal enough. I nodded and we said hello. Not sure if this is the place for small talk. We both know why we are here. And I am the new guy. Soon all of the chairs around the table are occupied and the psychiatrist comes in. The counselor from my intake hands a paper to each of us. We are asked to rate ourselves on a long list of symptoms and write our goals for the day. We are to share our top three symptoms with the psychiatrist.

Now, I have been in therapy for most of my adult life, but it has always been individual therapy. I've had lots of psychiatrist appointments but always just me and the psychiatrist. Sure, I've done personal growth work and men's groups where we sit in circles and share our challenges and hopes and dreams. But this was different. I was a mental patient now. We were all mental patients. I had to share my symptoms, talk about my medication, be vulnerable on day one, in front of all of these strangers.

But looking around the table at these people, these people that were about to know my secret, the one I worked so hard to conceal, they seemed nice enough, normal even, maybe just the right amount of crazy like me. After all, we were all here. We had to run the gauntlet of that first psychiatric interview. We were all brave.

Over the days to come I learned that the others were teachers and scientists and corporate executives and sales managers and undergraduate students and tech workers. They weren't so different from me. They had careers, children, degrees, responsibilities, ambitions, stress and also a mental illness. We had all recently had a breakdown. Most struggled with suicidal thoughts. A few had had recent attempts. Some came from the inpatient hospital, some had been referred by their doctor like me. All of us were at the end of our rope when we made the call about this program. But the end of the line was a new beginning now. And we were going there together.

The interesting thing about a day hospital program is that you don't have a cohesive cohort like with an outpatient group or classmates in a cohort in school. People rotate in and out every day. Each day we said goodbye to someone and were asked to say something nice about them, something positive about how they had aided in our recovery. The first day I barely knew the people that were leaving, but by my last day, when people said their goodbyes to me, I was the old guard. It was the people in the middle, that I spent a few days with on either end of their recoveries, that I found the most connection with. The ones that were just ahead of me were more comfortable and more vulnerable, which made it easier for me to open up.

The day was structured into multiple 45-minute groups during the day, punctuated by 15-minute breaks and a 30-minute lunch. We wrapped daily at 2:30. Every morning we wrote down our lunch order for the following day. The box lunches were delicious; to be honest lunch group turned out to be my favorite. I like hospital food.

Group Therapy

Every day started with the psychiatrist. We each went around and talked about our symptoms. He asked us questions and made recommendations, sometimes med changes. One day he held up a model of the brain and taught us about how it works. On another occasion he expounded on the biopsychosocial approach to treating mental illness. Basically there is no one-size fits all approach, everyone responds uniquely to different treatments, and meds aren't going to solve all your problems. These illnesses are complex and need a multifaceted treatment approach. You have to talk things out and change your habits and behavior too.

After that we went to process group, an open time for sharing, where we each got a chance to talk about what was going on for us, any insights we had made, and share the experiences that brought us here. The counselor at that group always had a box of Kleenex in their lap, at the ready in case a geyser of waterworks appeared, which was quite possible at any moment. I spoke of my struggles to hold it together, my feelings of fraud and my anger at some members of my family. I offered reassurance to others in the group. It was cathartic. We went through a lot of Kleenex.

Next came CBT group. That is short for cognitive behavioral therapy. We learned strategies for identifying and responding to negative cycles of thoughts, feelings, and behaviors. The most memorable part for me, which wasn't new, but was in need of review, was naming and responding to cognitive distortions like mind reading and jumping to conclusions and black and white thinking. Our minds have a tendency to go down many rabbit holes of negativity and it was helpful to learn some new skills to approach my thoughts differently.

Next came interpersonal therapy group, where we talked about boundaries and healthy communication and how to find balance and meaning in our relationships. Brene Brown, whose work on vulnerability I love, was frequently referenced. On Thursday family members were invited to come. I was able to publicly thank my wife for her support and ask her specifically for what I needed from her in my continued recovery; she did the same, praising my courage and offering her steadfast support. We held hands. We cried. Others brought spouses and friends and siblings. We all had so much support. We went through all the boxes of Kleenex on the conference table. There was a lot of love in that room.

The next group was life balance group. We talked about diet and exercise and meditation and priorities. My favorite part was the intersecting circles of health and work and leisure. It was good to be reminded that the work category encompasses more than just paid employment. It is childcare (and school drop off/pick up) and grocery shopping and paying bills. As I started writing down all that I was doing in a typical week I could see why I was so tired and my relationships were suffering. As responsible as I was, as many bills as I was paying and opportunities I was generating for the future, I was working or thinking about work, or doing work on the home front, most of my waking hours. All work and no play makes for a very sad boy.

The last meeting of the day was always wrap-up group. We had to make a plan for the afternoon and evening. On Friday we had to plan the whole weekend. We had to make sure to have structure and not too much vaguely planned downtime. Plans with close friends or family were encouraged, as was exercise. One of the counselors said that a lot of people got a haircut during the program because they realized they had been neglecting caring for themselves. I got a haircut.

One day we went on a field trip to the Japanese garden. We went in a big white van, the kind my friends and I used to take to soccer games or church retreats. I had recently rented one a similar size to move things into storage. The mental patients that tumbled out of this van certainly had baggage. I most remember the fish, the big koi. They were almost still under the water. Someone said that they don't move much in the winter to conserve energy. I felt like a koi that day, hibernating under water, conserving my energy until spring.

Vocation

The day I arrived at the day hospital I didn't want to be a therapist anymore. I didn't want to even say the word to the other participants about it. I didn't want them to think that I had some special magic that didn't really exist.

I am behind the curtain now and I can tell you that therapists are just as messed up as everyone else. Psychiatrists too. In my career now I have become friends with a lot of therapists, while continuing to see therapists for my own issues. I've learned what is painfully obvious now, but somehow as a kid my parents presented therapists like priests, magical exalted beings that maintain sacred space for baby boomers and their children. I suppose we do that, and are a little magical, but we are as broken as the rest of humanity. Sometimes more so.

Many of us mental health professionals had our own breakdowns and recovery and looked across the room at the kindred soul in front of us and thought, "I could do this, I'm good with people, I want to help people this way." We have mental health issues of our own. A rough childhood is a prerequisite for clinical licensure. That is why we are so good at connecting with those going through painful human experiences. We have been there ourselves. We have survived and come out whole. That is why we have the confidence that you can do it too. Get through this. And we have learned to hold space, the way others before us did for us. In addition to the acronyms after my name I have been trained in things like CBT, DBT, MI, ACT, SBIRT, with peerless leaders in the field like Hayes, Linehan, Harris, Robinson, and Wilson. They all have Dr. In front of their name, training I had considered but finally let go of. The GRE quantitative section and I never quite got along. But I do have some letters after my name. The counselors do too. I could tell that these counselors had that magic ability to connect.

Head Injury

In all of this quest for knowledge and legitimacy and effective treatment, the thing that I know works best is my ability to just be with someone. BE in the presence of pain. BE in the presence of suffering, grief, fear. Holding space for another person is a powerful gift to give. When my gut tells me to stop talking, stop offering solutions, put my clinician toolkit aside, and just BE (and I listen), that is when the magic happens. The tears flow, the deep dark thoughts and experiences never shared are brought to light, the wound is cleaned and readied for healing. This is when that toolbox of acronyms is best employed, once the wound is purged, but not necessarily healed.

I had a serious head injury many years ago in the Oregon desert. A friend and I had snuck off from a Halloween party to smoke cigarettes on the outskirts of my in-laws' ranch. I have never been a regular smoker, but it sounded like fun so I went along. I got out in front of my friend. We were talking and then I went silent. My friend found me unconscious 6 feet below where we had been walking. I had walked off some rim rock and slammed my head into a rock on the way down and landed in a sandy pit far below. I was knocked out. I woke up surrounded by people and covered in blood. Someone called for a doctor. Captain America was suddenly by my side, reporting for duty as the medical professional on call at the party. I was wrapped in bloody gauze from head to toe. My head hurt and my hand was numb. The superhero doctor determined that it was ok to move me, but that I should go to the hospital to get checked out and stitched up. My friend helped me to my feet and we proceeded to scare the hell out of all of the kids at the party. It was time for this blood soaked mummy to leave the costume party and go to the ER.

At the hospital, after the dried blood had been wiped away, the doctors and nurses carefully cleaned my wound. There was a lot of sand in there. They had to get it all for me to heal, every little grain, before they could stitch me up and send me off. It hurt like hell and it felt like it took forever, but the wound was clean. Being a therapist is kind of like that. The pent up tears and whispered words are like sand that must be exposed before healing can begin. At the hospital I got stitches, in my office I teach people skills with fancy names and acronyms and send them on their way. They come limping in and they go walking out. I used to believe with the right support and motivation, a person could heal all of their pain and trauma. Go back to normal as if nothing had ever happened. Like a broken leg after you return the crutches. At least if you don't look at the x-rays. I know now that that isn't true.

Traumatic experiences can never be erased from memory, old maladaptive patterns of behavior do come back when circumstances conspire to trigger pain that must be extinguished. What can change is our relationship to the pain, the memories, the thoughts. We can learn to let them go, to not be so pulled away from our lives, to walk outside no matter the weather. In the day hospital they called this the growth mindset. It is easy, when being diagnosed with a serious mental illness, especially one expected to last a lifetime, to feel that you are forever broken and must resign yourself to these same patterns of pain and relapse. But the psychiatrist at the day hospital reminded me that this isn't necessarily true. Sure, some people fall into that pattern, but others grow more mature, more aware of their triggers and ways to respond and get stronger and more resilient. Recovery comes sooner each time. We've learned how to get back up more gracefully.

I walked into this program feeling so broken. So sorry for myself. What a loser, what a fake, what a charlatan. I had cancelled appointments the week before with clients and patients because I couldn't do it. I was a fraud, I couldn't pretend to be a therapist anymore, especially when I knew how much more broken, unstable I was than them. I had nothing to offer them. Burned out, depressed, terrified. I just wanted to disappear.

The therapists at the day hospital were amazing. They were knowledgeable and energetic and empathetic and kind. In another circumstance they might have been colleagues or friends. They knew who I was, what I was, that I was one of them… at first I wondered if they were intimidated or nervous to be in front of a colleague that might be critiquing the work they typically do with people from other professions. It may be like a lawyer going to a lawyer or a doctor going to a doctor. Keeps you on your toes.

I wondered if they were as broken as I was. Did they know that I knew what was behind that curtain, that I knew what was behind that door that they came in and out of that was off limits to the patients? If I had a different professional background, I might imagine that that room was full of organic vegetables and bean bag chairs and group hugs and deep deep thoughts on the human soul. I'm sure it is more likely filled with computers and messy desks and dry treatment team meetings. But the unicorns are still in there. In and out, in and out they flutter. They trade off leading groups and pulling people for one-on-ones. Thank god for these unicorns. In hindsight these thoughts distracted me probably more than they distracted them. They became teachers, some of them I wished were my friends and colleagues. I wanted their passion for the work, their knowledge, their strength despite sitting in the daily presence of so much pain. I wanted it to rub off on me. And it did.

I have heard that a fair amount of people go to therapy and may have the fleeting thought "I could do this, I could be a therapist, I'm good with people and interested in psychology, I like to listen, my corporate job is meaningless and I want to help people." Some leave it at that and forget and go back to their not-expected-to-be-magical life. Others do research online or call their therapist friends and interrogate them. I have had this conversation with several friends. I usually talk them out of it. The expense and many years of training, to come out to uncertain income in exchange for swallowing the pain of humanity. No thanks, they take the off-ramp. I certainly tried not to do this, but it didn't let me go. I followed the path, often kicking and screaming. Screenwriter, non-profit administrator, actor, chef, documentary filmmaker, the list goes on. I went down each of these roads and found dead ends, or maybe only hobbies I would resume later. I cook for my family, serve on a non-profit board, occasionally work on my screenplay, and dream of performing again in community theatre in retirement. I do a lot of public speaking now, I suppose that might qualify as performance art, though Powerpoints and the finer points of evidence-based psychotherapies aren't quite Shakespeare. I'm not sure about those identities, but as much as I am questioning it, I am definitely a therapist.

I watched these amazing unicorns at the top of their game, practicing their craft. "I could do that," I thought. "I could be that good...or maybe I am that good." On my best day maybe. But, unlike most of the patients in this room I didn't need to go back to graduate school to be a therapist. I didn't need to have years of training or take any tests or pay any money. I had already paid my dues. I could just go right back to it. But I was still thinking I might have to quit, or take a longer break, or whatever. Keep avoiding the inevitable. I still wanted to run away and never come back.

I have fantasized about being an Uber driver or flipping pancakes at IHOP. Those guys seem pretty chill. Anything but be a therapist again. But here I was, feeling that spark, that pull.

Maybe, by the end of this program, maybe, just maybe I can be a therapist again. I became curious. It was like grad school all over again, but I felt unqualified to even be there, like that depressed undergraduate very far from making it in the world, certainly any career. Maybe, just maybe, if I made it to graduation day I might get to be an adult, stop pretending and do what I was meant to do. I went home, had dinner with my family, kissed my wife and daughters goodnight, took my medication, crawled into bed, watched a crime drama on my iPhone, and fell asleep by 8pm. I was exhausted but looking forward to another day. They were holding space for me at the day hospital.

Throughout the program they referenced a bio-psycho-social approach to treatment. It was a good refresher on the core tenets of the approach I was taught in grad school. It deeply informs the approach I continue to take in my work. Basically, mental illness is complicated. To treat it, and prevent it, multiple parts of a human's being must be addressed.

Bio, or biological, means brain and body and genetics. If I don't exercise and don't eat right and drink too much and my parents and grandparents had a mental illness, then I'm vulnerable to one too.

Psycho means psychological, or what is going on in my head: thoughts and feelings and behaviors, how I respond to the world around me, and how my stories about the past impact how I relate to the world now, including how I relate to myself.

Social means just that, social. How do I connect with other people, what is the quality of my relationships, how do I fit into my community? In social work this is described as a "person-in-environment" perspective. No one lives in a vacuum; we are all deeply impacted by the people and world that we interact with on a daily basis.

The bio-psycho-social model sounds interesting, a bit academic, a bit clean and clinical, but when I try to parse my life and my experience into those boxes it becomes a bit difficult. Life, history, memories are blurry and incomplete and not so easy to categorize. But I try. I think about it constantly. What led me here? Why do I have this illness? There is no doubt my genetic inheritance is triggered by the stressful environment I am living in. My brain is a loaded gun waiting to go off, but I am learning that I have a choice of how close I want to hold onto that story. The day hospital isn't about sorting through the wreckage of the past. We will get to that later. It is about making a plan and building skills to live a good life today, in the here and now. That's exactly where I needed to bring my attention.

They told me my last day in the program would be on a Tuesday. Seven days and they were sending me home. I wasn't sure if that was what they thought I needed or what my insurance said it would pay for. It certainly didn't feel like enough. I wasn't better. It had been an overall good weekend, some friends visited, I played with my kids and watched a few movies, and I slept a lot. I was withdrawn but relatively social, but certainly not my upbeat self. I texted my friends a link about the day hospital program so that I didn't have to talk much about it.

Monday morning I was feeling scared. I didn't shave or shower. I pulled a hoodie over my unshaven face and covered my tousled hair with a ball cap. There were new people in the group that morning. Others had left last week, the ones I felt close to, the ones that were as crazy as me but also normal enough, they were gone. Replaced by strangers. It was disorienting. I felt alone. I wasn't ready to go. I didn't want to go. I was just getting in my groove here, finding a rhythm and a routine. I liked the counselors and the psychiatrist. I couldn't face my life, not how it was. I wasn't ready to go back to it. This had become a safe place for me but now I had to leave.

The pit of despair opened and I hung my legs over the edge and peered down. That black door was open once again. I would rather die than keep living the lie that I had been living, struggling to be good when I was far from fine. I decided to be honest when I rated how I was feeling. Maybe I could stay longer. After I shared, everyone in the room avoided eye contact but the psychiatrist, who confirmed that these were just thoughts and I had no clear plan or intention to hurt myself. One of the counselors later pulled me out to talk about it. They moved on to the next person. The next day, when I said goodbye and people said their nice thing about me, a few said that my honesty about my suicidal thoughts had been a turning point for them. They had been underreporting and struggling quietly, but my opening up about it—and not being thrown right in the hospital—helped them feel safer in sharing how deep their dark thoughts were. That is what I hope for these words I am writing. That as self-shattering as these stories are, I hope that they can be of some help.

By the end of that Monday, the day before I left, I felt better, stronger, clearer that maybe I could make it.

The last day I met alone with the psychiatrist and made a plan to transition back to my outpatient treatment providers. He encouraged continued therapy and focusing on more time alone with my wife. He said I shouldn't work more hours than my peers, which I'm not sure is a great measuring stick since I work in healthcare. I had a few more days off. I planned the rest of my week, a hike with friends, an afternoon with my daughter, a weekday matinee movie date with my wife. I was far from 100% but feeling hopeful and had some direction. I planned to carry my slim navy blue notebook of handouts around with me wherever I went. In fact, I did carry it with me, in my briefcase or backpack or car, wherever I went for two months after discharge. I rarely opened it, but it was a security blanket, an instruction manual from the unicorns in case I got jammed up. It is still on my desk in my home office. I'm not ready to put it on the shelf yet.

As we got up to leave after the last group I felt a strong urge to hug the counselor and the people next to me that I had known for a few days. But this wasn't that type of place. I nodded politely and packed up my bag and slipped out the door.

A song that my dad had on regular rotation in the Paul Simon playlist that was the soundtrack to my childhood slid across my mind. "Hey Siri," I yell in the general direction of my Blue-tooth-linked iPhone, "PLAY GUMBOOTS!" Asking my smart assistant to do something is like talking to my spouse in the other room, repeating myself at progressively higher volume until understood. But miraculously, the song started playing through the Jeep's speakers.

The familiar acoustic guitar washes over me. I am transported to a house in the woods where I learned how to cook and how to drive and how to live. Long before I ever knew what divorce or trauma or suicide or breakdown meant, I knew the words to this song. I imagine Paul Simon sitting next to me, the friend he sings about in his song.

"... breakdowns come and breakdowns go... what are you going to do about it, that's what I want to know...?"

The sun stretched out over the water. I drove over the bridge, leaving the day hospital one last time. Tears streamed down my face as my lips sang along to the familiar tune. I punched the accelerator, the Jeep thundering over the wide floating bridge, a tingle surging through me. It was time to go home and live.

2

Identity

This book is about identity. I am still trying to figure out who I am and what I am all about. I also struggle with taking up space to tell this story. There are plenty of memoirs by white men. We need more diverse literary voices. I want to read more memoirs from people of color and women and LGBTQ individuals. Those stories need to be told, and are being told, but deserve to be shared more widely. But those are their stories. This is mine. And I need to share it. This is my story of becoming a man. Yes, this is a memoir from a cisgender heterosexual American man of European descent. This is also the story of a bipolar redheaded stepchild who grew up in in a rural community. This is the story of a successful professional with an invisible disability. When you look under the hood, the story is more nuanced than being able to claim (or have claimed for me) simply "white man" as my identity.

This is the story of a boy with two fathers, one bipolar, one transgender. Of a child with a long family history, a genetic inheritance, of serious mental illness. A boy raised by a single mother, poor by the standard of their affluent neighbors. A boy whose brother ran away and returned a ghost. It is the story of loss, of suicide attempts and completions. It is the story of a personal battle with depression not won, but accepted. A heart healed but not unbroken. Like the Japanese art called *kintsugi* of gluing broken bowls together with gold: the cracks remain, but something beautiful bonds with the jagged edges.

This is my story. I hope by sharing it, by being this deeply vulnerable, that it will help you too, my dear reader. No matter what we look like or where we come from, at the core, the pain and triumph of being human is universal.

3

Warning Signs

High Dive

My freshman year of college a kid jumped out of his seventh-floor window, spilling his brains and body all over the concrete below. I lived on the seventh floor. Thankfully he and I didn't share the same view. I had seen him making ramen noodles in the dorm kitchen just that evening. I had avoided small talk. The guy was awkward and aloof, and I suppose so was I. I now wish I had said something, made small talk, anything to have interrupted ramen being his last meal. A few short hours later his lifeless body was covered by a blue tarp, blood running along the sidewalk in a seeming unending trail. The police were knocking on doors, asking all kinds of questions. Their questions felt like an interrogation, some insinuation that me or one of my friends had pushed him. What a terrifying thought to have to consider. Now that I've watched a lot of cop shows I see why they talked to us like that...ruling out all the possibilities.

I called my mother, to assure her that I was ok, not to worry. This felt like the most momentous thing that had ever happened so I assumed that it must be all over the news. She hadn't heard a word about it. I didn't realize that while murders are often sensationalized, suicide is not something people want to cuddle up with their morning coffee or TV dinner tray. Celebrity deaths would be the exception. My mom had no idea why I was sobbing on the other end of the line. I couldn't get it out. After I finally caught my breath and wiped my tears, I told her what had happened. She was sweet and reassuring and encouraged me to come home for the weekend. After I hung up the phone I sat trembling, feeling so alone surrounded by the cement block walls of the dorm room that I shared with only my own thoughts. I was so deeply shaken, beyond the clear terror of seeing a dead body outside, because my own melancholy frightened me. It was a fog that seldom lifted that year. Like the rain outside in a Pacific Northwest winter, ever present, even if just a drizzle.

Despite my dark moods, I had never even seriously considered suicide. Maybe a fleeting thought here or there, but never a plan or a sustained focus on it. At the time I hoped that I never would have those thoughts again, felt that maybe others got that sad and hopeless, but I never would. Soon after, spring arrived and the dark thoughts were replaced by optimism of good times ahead. They were already revealing themselves in the summer dandelions popping up near the blood that never quite washed out of that sidewalk.

I hoped that I would leave that tortured darkness behind with the other melancholy I experienced in that dorm, but it turned out that was just the beginning of that dark road. My life would continue to be deeply impacted by suicide.

Since that dark day in my dorm I have struggled with some

very intense bouts of depression, often punctuated by a baseline of deep anxiety and racing thoughts that vacillate between my grandiose plans to save the world from its problems and my deep-seated feelings of worthlessness and despair. I have had dark moments of my own that threatened to cut my life short. I am grateful that I have lived to tell the tale.

Y2K

I started my sophomore year in the fall of the new millennium, or Y2K as the newscasters and doomsdayers liked to call it. The world, it turned out, had not come to an end when the clocks rolled over. The computers still worked and life went on.

I had started the fall quarter excited to be back at college. Freshman year had had its ups and downs, but I was glad to be back on campus as a sophomore. I was nursing a broken heart. I couldn't stop ruminating about the girl I had dated in the spring who had broken up with me before summer. I sometimes still ran into her on campus. Every time I saw her I felt like I was being punched in the gut. The intensive political economy program I had selected was harder than I expected. The reading was dense and the Marxist professors were extremely cynical about the state of the world. I lived in an on-campus apartment-style dorm with some of my friends from freshman year, but we all seemed to have our own thing going. That feeling of community from my big co-ed dorm floor wasn't the same here. I spent a lot of time alone.

As the days got shorter, the skies darkened, and so did my thoughts. I started skipping class. I avoided eye contact anytime I left my room. I didn't ever want to see that girl again; it was too painful. One day I looked up at the balcony that had been a high dive just the year before. It made sense to me now. Why he had jumped. I was out of other options, no more distraction seemed suitable. food, alcohol, sex. Nothing mattered. That fall quarter of my sophomore year I started to withdraw from my life. Depression was pulling me deeper. I didn't like to drink alone, only at parties; I didn't like drugs, marijuana made me feel silly but then slow and dumb and anxious and irritable. I just wanted to be alone. Nothing could distract me from the voices, the thoughts that I was worthless, would never amount to anything. They were too important, these thoughts of mine. My brain was screaming obscenities at me all the time. My life was over. I stopped going to class. I barely left my room. I was rail thin.

The First Pill

I was home for the holidays and my mom could tell something was seriously wrong. She urged me to go to the doctor, saying maybe they could give me something mild to help me feel better. I was very resistant, but I went. I saw a nurse practitioner who had me fill out a rating form for my symptoms of depression. Her eyes grew large as I circled the severe end of most categories. She offered to prescribe something called a Selective Serotonin Reuptake Inhibitor, or SSRI. Basically it is supposed to treat depression by keeping more good feelings, serotonin, bopping around in your brain, letting you soak up a bit more positivity before they cycle through your synapses again. Little did I know at the time, but this blockbuster class of drugs was new to the market and the pharmaceutical companies were promoting them heavily. There had probably been a pharma rep in that clinic the day before, handing out samples, coaching the providers on just what to say if someone scored high on the depression scale.

I was resistant but she was insistent. Suddenly my prolonged sadness was a sickness. This seemed like the end of the line, a last ditch effort, a hail Mary. She prescribed Paxil and asked me to stay in touch.

I went back to school. The diarrhea was terrible and I felt off, hard to describe how. My thoughts flew faster and got darker. Suicidal thoughts went from fleeting to constant.

Blood Bath

I awoke in a tub full of lukewarm water. Groggy and inebriated, immediately nauseated. I heaved and vomited into the still water. I could see pills, lots of pills, and the tacos I had had for lunch. There was also blood in the water. I was suddenly terrified, as if there were sharks circling and my life was in imminent danger. My life was in danger. A bloody razor blade was next to the soap dish on the edge of the tub. I reflexively stood up, wiping the blood and water and vomit away with my hand.

Shivering, I stepped out of the tub, almost tripping on a half empty bottle of cheap vodka. The irony was lost on me, then, but not now. To survive a suicide attempt but die by hitting my head on the tub because I tripped and fell back into a tub full of blood and vomit and drowned in my own failure to even get suicide right. That would be ironic.

I wrapped a towel around me and walked into the dark hall. I pulled the long cord of the phone we shared in my dorm back into the bathroom. I slid to the floor, clutching the phone for dear life. My wet hair dripped pink, blood-stained water onto my freckled knees. I called my therapist. I didn't know who else to call. I was terribly embarrassed and as public as my suicide would have been, I had no interest in anyone knowing about this almost-suicide that wasn't. No answer. I called again. No answer. 911 would call too much attention. I kept dialing my therapist. I looked up at the counter and saw all of the boxes and bottles of pills I had ingested. Mostly over-the-counter but some prescription. The lid to the bottle of vodka that I had borrowed from my roommate's stash. I was never much of a drinker but alcohol was always around, despite being only 19. It was a college dorm after all. My friend's shaving case was there too. Zipped open on the counter. There was a base and several straight razors, but one was missing. My buddy was old-school and he liked his whiskers trimmed with a straight razor. I was drunk, scared, and part of me still wanted to die. Some of those containers still had pills in them. There was more vodka in the freezer. I could try again. This nightmare could be over.

Then the phone rang. It was my therapist. He had been confused why his caller ID had blown up with a name he didn't recognize. My roommate's mom paid for the line so it was in her name. He finally got curious and called back. "What's going on?" He asked directly after recognizing my muffled voice saying hello when I answered. "I'm ummm.... I did something stupid... I drank vodka and took pills and I am bleeding and I don't know what to do." A brief silence followed. "Can you call 911? You should call 911. You need to go to the hospital." A longer silence followed. "No," I finally said, as resolutely as I could. "I don't want anyone to know." I had seen ambulances come for other kids, when they drank too much or who knows what else. It was the talk of the campus for days. I thought of the morning after that boy's jump from the dorm my freshman year. I would go to the hospital, but I wanted to go quietly.

He agreed to pick me up and drive me himself after I assured him that I had stopped bleeding and could stand on my own. I dried off and shoved all of the pill bottles into the trash. I wiped off the razor blade and put it back with the shaving kit in my roommate's drawer. I picked up the vodka bottle and dried the bathroom floor as best I could. I crept down the hall to my room and pulled on a hoodie and jeans and running shoes. I pulled a hat over my dripping wet hair. I grabbed the garbage from the bathroom and headed out the front door. I threw it in the nearby dumpster and recycled the vodka bottle.

I stumbled down the sidewalk. Sometimes it isn't until closing time comes, when you get kicked out of the bar, that you notice how drunk you really are. The sober night air clung to my wet skin. I was underdressed for a rainy fall night. I nodded to another student that stumbled by, avoiding eye contact. It was not unusual for a kid to be stumbling home drunk at 3 am on this campus. I was incognito. I reached the main road just as my therapist's forest green Saturn sedan pulled to the stop sign across the street. I waved and crossed in front of his car. He slowed and looked closer at me. Probably confirming that I was the correct crazy person to let into his car. He unlocked the door and I climbed in. Suddenly I felt safe, very safe. My nervous system had kicked into flight when I woke up in the tub and I had fought myself this far. I was relieved to let someone else get me the rest of the way to the hospital.

By the time I arrived I was no longer scared but in a silly inebriated state. I hear I am a fun drunk. I get very very friendly, in a good way. Similar to when I've come out of anesthesia from surgery, suddenly everyone in the hospital was my new best friend. Suddenly I was trying to network, asking if people knew my aunt, a nurse at the hospital. They stitched up my wrist and wiped away the rest of the blood and vomit.

Hours later, long after the sun had come up, I awoke under a hospital blanket in a thin gown, the harsh lights of the ER burning my eyes. Saying I was sober was an understatement. My escapades of the previous evening were coming back to me in bits and pieces. I was scared and confused. What the hell happened? How did it come to this? The inside of my wrist burned. I saw a nurse looking in my direction through the thin curtain that separated me from the ER. I heard her pick up the phone, saying "Please page social work, that psych patient is awake." She looked nervous. I felt totally harmless. Not even a danger to myself. I had never thought of myself as a "psych patient" before.

Soon the social worker came in. I remember him being a serious man, probably in his mid forties, with a dark brown moustache. His demeanor was cold and unsympathetic but somehow reassuring, in a very serious paternal way. I could tell he wanted to help, but he couldn't get too close. I now know exactly what that feels like, to be on the other side of this assessment when you have already witnessed so much pain and tragedy in your career. You keep your distance. I could tell he cared though, especially as time went on. He realized pretty quickly that I was a mixed-up college kid that had had a really bad night. I wasn't that crazy. I swore up and down that I wouldn't do it again. He believed me, even if I didn't. He said I wouldn't qualify to go into a psych hospital, even if I went voluntarily. I wasn't crazy enough, not a danger to anyone at all, again not even me. Maybe they didn't have a day hospital in this town.

He said to me, "Make up your mind and do what you're going to do. If you're going to be in school, fine; if not, fine, but it's not acceptable to take your own life." He was really serious about that last point. I took the lecture to heart.

He offered me a bus ticket home to my dorm. I was shocked. I had just had a suicide attempt, or lack thereof, and they were putting me on a bus? I felt so vulnerable. He had called my mom, but she was several hours away. My younger brothers still lived at home and she couldn't leave them alone. She had encouraged me to come home but we had yet to work out the transportation. I called a friend that I knew could keep a secret.

When I walked into my dorm my roommate looked at me suspiciously. "What happened to you last night?" In my drunken state I thought that I had cleaned up, but the bathroom was a mess and his vodka was missing. He spotted the bandage on my wrist. He knew before I even said anything. We sat on the couch and I told him what happened, what I could remember anyway. He looked really freaked out, the color draining from his face. Basically the hospital had released me home…with him. I tried to reassure him that I was fine, that it wouldn't happen again. That it wasn't his responsibility to look after me. To his credit, he refused to leave me alone until we made a plan. He borrowed our roommate's car and drove me home.

And that was it. I kept it contained. My mental illness is shared only on a need-to-know basis. The secret mission to keep me alive, keep up the illusion that he is a normal guy. I quietly slipped away from college with little fanfare, I suppose not so differently than this most recent incident that led me to the day hospital. It certainly didn't get as far as that bloody scene in the bathtub, but my plotting mind was leading me down that path again. This time, as that, I quietly took a break from my responsibilities. That break from my studies lasted a year and a half before I returned to school. This time around my FMLA ran out in two weeks. Somehow the two weeks feels longer. Good thing this town has a day hospital.

Songbirds

In 2011 the world lost a beautiful woman that I loved very dearly. My cousin took her own life. She was 23. She was a dancer and an actress and had the most beautiful voice you ever heard. She was smart and hilarious and kind and so beautiful, with dark eyes and long auburn hair that draped over her slender figure. Her eyes were full of sparks of fire and pools of sadness.

She was hospitalized after experiencing a very intense period of mania. Since being released she had been struggling to accept the reality of bipolar disorder in her life, symptoms of which had been present for years, but now had a name (with all of the stigma that comes along with it). I had been noticing the signs but kept my concerns to myself. I took her to lunch after she got out of the hospital. She said she hated the meds. She was tired and feeling flat and gaining weight. I encouraged her to not make any changes too fast. I encouraged her to stay connected to her mental health providers. She didn't have a care team that she trusted. She stopped taking her meds and self-medicated with marijuana and cocaine. Over the weeks that followed her family struggled to know what to do with the monstrous depression that took her by force, and then tied that noose around her neck. Her younger brother found her dangling there. He cut her down and tried CPR, but it was too late. I showed up just as the coroner was loading her body in the truck...the grief in that house was unbearable, as her parents and siblings grappled with the raw wounds that ripped open the moment her pain in this life ended. Their pain was just beginning.

I awoke sobbing the next morning. My pregnant wife and I decided to take the day off and visit my hometown. My mother had been out of state caring for my grandfather, who had recently had a stroke, but I wanted to see my brother and grandmother. In recent years I had distanced myself emotionally from those two, protecting my heart from what have at times been painful relationships to maintain. My grandmother was hospitalized earlier that year after swallowing some pills and narrowly avoiding what would have been the end of a lifelong battle with major depression. My brother had just moved home from California, a place where he was finally able to get appropriate treatment for his schizoaffective disorder and substance abuse issues. He continues to experience ongoing psychosis, frequently conversing with invisible characters, but he has also finally come home to us, which a few years ago I had all but given up hope of ever happening. We went out for Chinese. The fried rice and mu shu pork were good, the vegetables were soggy. My heart was not wide open, but it was present as I hugged them goodbye and told them I loved them. I was so glad we were all alive.

Conviction

A week later I was driving home from work, feeling so aware of my exhaustion. I was tired, frustrated with the feeling that despite all of the health changes I have made in my life, I still don't have a lot of energy. I revisited my frequent worry that the lethargy, the brain fog, and the subtle cognitive delays that I experience would hinder my ability to achieve my goals. There are many factors involved, but a key piece of this is the mood-stabilizing medication that I take every day. I was taking less than I used to, and had cautiously (and under medical supervision) lowered the dose a bit recently, but had chosen to be pretty conservative about any big reductions, especially with the level of stress that I was under. Better safe than sorry seems to be the default, even if it seems like there is some part of me that is numbed out to life, to the expansive energy that might be possible if I was drug-free. For me, I choose to take a pill every day, not to ignore or hide from my problems, but to humbly accept that for today anyway, this is a tool that helps me to be present and alive in the world. It is a fucking bitter pill, but let me tell you when I woke up that morning to the reality that my cousin was dead and gone...I took my medication and chose life.

I sobbed so hard that I struggled to catch my breath—choking and coughing, my grief triggering a visceral reminder of my own trauma. My own neck. I thought of my cousin's beautiful-swan like neck, she always had this glow about her. I remember wrestling as kids, pinning her shoulders to the ground. She laughed and shot her hands to my neck and I was thrown off. We were both on our backs laughing. Now as I struggled to catch my breath, I imagined that moment when she tried to catch her last breath, but she couldn't. Her executioner had carried out the death sentence.

I too had been convicted and sentenced to death once. Preparations had been made. I was all alone in a house in the woods with a 2nd floor deck. I went to the hardware store. I bought a rope and spent weeks perfecting the noose from diagrams on the internet. It was the real thing. I built my own gallows. Finally the moment had come. I stood in the night air, my breath visible. I counted them and smiled. Finally at peace. These were to be my last breaths. With a calm certainty I stepped onto the chair and looped the noose over my head. I wasn't scared at all. This was what had to happen. I was clear. This was the answer, no other way out than to end it.

I kicked the chair away and felt the air suck out of my lungs. The rope tightened, pinching every part of my neck it bore into. Just moments before I had acted with the smooth certainty of an executioner, but now every part of my being wanted to breathe again. I was terrified, dangling scared. I didn't want to die. Instinct, or something, kicked in, and an eternity later I somehow managed to get a toehold on the chair and inch it back over, until it could bear my weight. When the rope loosened I breathed deep. I coughed and choked. I was so disoriented. I ran away from that gallows to a safer place where I would not be left alone. I got help and I recovered and it has never been that bad again. But I keep a close eye on it.

I wonder if my cousin had that moment, that moment where she tried to take it back, but maybe couldn't. For some reason I could. If that chair had gone three inches farther away, I would not have been able to pull it back. Someone else would be telling you this story. My wife's daughters would have someone else's eyes.

I continue to have a fear that if the depression gets bad enough it will happen again, and when it did happen again that fear grew greater still. Sleeping every night with your attempted murderer, he's never far away. You have forgiven him, let him live with you, but can you ever trust him? Can you trust yourself? I can say with certainty that the odds that I will kill another person are quite low. The odds of me murdering myself? A bit higher.

I think about these experiences I have had a lot, but I am very private about them. I carry a tremendous amount of shame and sadness around the subject of mental illness. I sometimes hope to one day not need to take medication to keep my brain in balance, a day that may come someday... but after looking into the grief-soaked eyes of my aunt who had just lost her youngest daughter, I came home, took my meds, and called to tell my mother how much I love her. I distinctly remember standing in the bathroom alone, sobbing, my tattered heart coming apart at the seams once more. I leaned back on the wall and slid to the floor, my face buried in my hands. I must go on. This was the end of a chapter, but also the beginning of a new one.

After my own escape from the gallows, and as the rope burn on my neck began to heal, my psychiatrist recommended we try a new medication: lithium. It was a scary step up from the antidepressants I had been taking, but despite several trials, they seemed to be making me feel worse, not better. I remember it distinctly...a week or so later I woke up and I no longer wanted to die. I looked around and could acknowledge the wreckage of my life, but the racing thoughts that were so insistent that I must perish—were gone. I began to pick up the pieces of my life. I finished school, I got married, I started a job that quickly turned into a career. I also gained 75 pounds and struggled every day with the fear that I would lose my mind again, haunted by the need to prove to myself and everyone around me that I was "ok" and was finally living up to the potential that had been so rudely interrupted all of those years ago. In the last couple of years I have made a lot of changes, some visible on the outside, but more than anything on the inside. I switched to a med with fewer side effects, spent a lot of time in therapy, and joined a men's group. I found people that I allowed to see past my facade. People that loved and respected the real me, warts and all.

Some say that our deepest purpose comes from our deepest pain, others say it is from our deepest joy. Mental illness has carved a deep impression on my heart, and as I try to sort through what I want to focus on in my work, my dear cousin's death has profoundly impacted the path I continue to be on. After the funeral I went home, loosened my tie, took my medication, and rested my hand on my wife's round belly. I felt my unborn daughter kick for the first time. Life is a blessing.

Double Jeopardy

A few months later I visited my cousin's mother in a psychiatric hospital near my home. Her depression since her daughter's death had brought her to her knees. She was in a very dark place. I remember sitting outside with her at a picnic table on a cool day; she tried to smile, but her eyes were so tired and sad. Hollowed out with grief. We talked about hospital food and how our pregnancy was going. She spoke of her daughter in the present tense, and then caught herself. Her daughter was in the past tense now. A tear rolled down her face. At the time I was grieving my own loss and was certainly empathetic to her struggle, but I couldn't really comprehend the depth of her pain until I was a parent myself. A few months later when I held my daughter for the first time, a tear rolled down my cheek and my heart doubled in size. My children have carved out a very large space in my heart. I can only imagine the darkness that would fill that void if they died so young, so tragically.

A week after my aunt was released from the hospital, she

walked to the bridge near her house and jumped. The policeman who had first arrived when my cousin died was first on the scene and knew exactly who she was. Poor guy. He was first on the scene for both suicides. Now my beautiful aunt was gone too. Two angels who would no longer sing beautiful duets together again. I like to imagine they are singing with the other angels in heaven. I don't know if there is such a place, but if there is, they are most certainly there, surrounded by love.

A few years later I started working for the hospital system that had cared for my aunt before she died. It wasn't a conscious choice to apply based on that experience, it just happened that they had a good job available and I needed one. Near the end of that first year I had an opportunity to lead suicide assessment training for all of the providers in the medical group. Our team of social workers, psychologists, and psychiatrists worked with these front-line doctors and nurse practitioners to get more comfortable asking the right questions and providing protocols and resources for how to respond if someone wasn't safe to walk out of their office. This approach was proven to reduce death by suicide, as many people who complete suicide have had contact with a healthcare professional in the month before their death, usually a primary care provider. Again, I didn't plan it as some sort of absolution for missing the signs, but it was something.

Our fragmented healthcare system failed my aunt and cousin. I was glad to be able to offer my skills and experience to ensure that it was less likely to happen to anyone else's daughter or cousin or aunt or mother. It felt good, I felt relieved. I was off the hook. Maybe I could do something else with my life now besides try to repair the whole mental health system. I did my part.

It turned out I would have opportunities to do a whole lot more to improve our broken system. I'm on a zero suicide workgroup where we are redesigning care across a seven-state health system to make sure that people's care in this area is more consistent and aligned with what we know works to keep people alive. I also have to continue to confront my own demons, again and again, along the way.

Dark Reflections

I wonder how many suicide attempts happen like mine. Incomplete. I've been trained not to say someone "committed suicide." It isn't a crime you commit. It is also discouraged to say "completed suicide." It isn't necessarily something that is finally finished after multiple attempts. But it is a task that has a finality to it. A life is over. "Died by suicide" is preferable language, but not one I ever hope to say again about anyone. In my career now I have heard many stories of people's suicide attempts. Sometimes I am the only one they've ever told about it. It is one of life's most private, darkest and most shameful moments. Not something you talk about at cocktail parties or job interviews. When you don't die, sometimes no one ever knows. The rope breaks, the belt snaps, you throw up the pills. You just go on living and no one knows. If you died that would be another story, you have given up control of the narrative then, but that is the consolation prize of living. You are still writing your own story.

Like suicide attempts, miscarriages happen frequently but are rarely spoken of. This has been my experience, on both fronts. My wife had one on our journey to full-term pregnancy. My sister and my sisters-in-law had them too. But most people don't know. It isn't talked about. We keep this close. Unless you lose the baby full-term — then everyone knows. Like the woman I used to work with who lost her twins 8 months into pregnancy. She posted on Facebook about it. It was so heartbreaking. People found out about my cousin's suicide on Facebook. What an impersonal place to find out such personal news. Like walking by a bulletin board and seeing a picture of your friend posted, your first notification of their tragic end writ large for all to see.

That first time I tried to die, I had never seen a dead body. The next spring my paternal grandfather died. Parkinson's and old age took him to heaven in his 80s. At least that's where I figure he is, as he and my grandmother were very very Catholic.

I remember his crinkled hands and gray skin and brown suit, wedged into the wooden coffin. He was an old man. The way it is supposed to be. Also, I wasn't there when he died, so it wasn't as real. I was in the next room when my wife's mom died, but I didn't see her go. I was there for my grandmother's last breath. I was holding her hand. I was also sitting with my sister-in-law when she exhaled for the last time. Neither were particularly young or healthy, but both were unexpected.

Suicide for me has never been about death. It is about escape. It is about feeling trapped with no way out but to end the game. Take your chances with what comes next, because whatever it is it couldn't be more terrifying than the daily dark confrontation with your own demons. Whatever life you had, you imagined you had, feels like it's behind thick glass, and you are out in the yard shivering without a key to get back in. When life feels like it is out of options, you start looking for death.

Our brains are problem-solving machines, and suicide is a tempting ultimate solution. If you can't fix it, pull the plug and take your chances. Shutting down and rebooting my computer works when it is going haywire, so why not the body? Well, it turned out I didn't need to physically die to shed myself of the demons that had me hiding in the corner. To reboot. But something had to die. The word *crisis* has its origin in Greek, meaning "decision point." I needed to change, not just go back to the status of barely holding on, white-knuckling it through a neverending rainstorm. I had to make a decision. It wasn't to pretend that my symptoms didn't exist and keep struggling to live anyway. Mental illness is real, but before recovery can come, acceptance brings you to your knees. It was painful to accept that I was sick and I needed help. I also had to accept that I needed to change how I was living if I wanted to keep on living. I am so grateful that I have had the opportunity to heal. I am so glad to be breathing.

4

Origins

Grandma

The vanilla ice cream was melted by the time I ladled it with
a plastic spoon into her sweet crinkled mouth. "Do you want
something to eat?" the nurse asked. "More ice cream," she said
with a sleepy smile. We all smiled. I went back to dutifully
pouring the cool liquid down her parched throat. Still dry from
the tube that was in her throat just hours before, she was grateful for the sweet relief.

Her frail body tucked tightly into the hospital bed, my grandmother's dark eyes were still piercing. Her salt and pepper hair
crowned her soft features. She launched into a story about the
Inuit and the Yupik, whom she insisted she had helped broker a
truce between. I felt sorry for the hospital staff that thought she

was off her rocker.

In fact, she had made history once upon a time. I smiled, secretly wondering if this was a sign of her drifting toward dementia, but knowing that one day she probably had participated in such diplomacy. I asked her to tell me the story, and it became clear that she was recalling her time on the Senate Indian Affairs committee. She had spoken of it often when I spent time with her in my youth. In her current state, the 1970s probably felt like just this afternoon. I had a feeling that while in the twilight of surgery she may have drifted back to that time, a time of purpose and connection. A time when she was valued and influential. Before she was a poor old lady with a broken hip.

She straightened up and looked at me with those piercing eyes. She interrogated me about my work and insisted that at 32, I shouldn't be bored. She said my hair was too short, she missed my curls. She had been paying attention and she knew exactly where she was. She dazzled me with that sharp memory. I felt a sweet calm come over me, a comfort I had not felt with my grandmother for years. I felt safe and clear in my role. I came to feed her ice cream and make a plan for her discharge and recovery. I was her sweet and loving boy once again.

My mind flashed to the last time I visited her in the hospital, a few years before. Sitting at the end of her bed staring at a newspaper, I could barely look at her. That day I could barely contain my terror and my rage. The geriatric psychiatric unit is not a place for grandchildren, even adult ones.

Overwhelmed and alone, she had swallowed a bottle of pills but lived to tell the tale, as she had several times before. I had struggled with similar demons and I knew the sick hold that depression could have on a mind. I think that is why I was so afraid; the line between sanity and sickness is one I had long struggled to stay on the right side of. It runs in the family.

But this time was different; she was just a sweet old lady who had fallen down. This time I could stroke her hair and listen to

her stories and complaints about the medical staff. This time I
felt safe and in control.

I heard the giggles of my wife and daughter as they came to
fetch me for bedtime. It was time to go. The nurse came in and
slipped a syringe full of morphine into Grandma's IV and her
eyes started to flutter. I kissed her head and stroked her hair. As
I walked out the door I glanced back and smiled. I imagined she
was back in Alaska brokering peace among the native peoples.

My grandmother had chronic depression. She had a suicide attempt when I was a little boy. I remember driving to California
with Dad in a moving truck so that she could be closer to us. I
didn't know this bubbly woman pattering my cheeks with pink
lipstick had downed a bottle of pills just days before.

When she reached her 90s, she made it clear that she was done,
but would let life take its course. She made me her power of attorney and made her wishes clear. I wept when I spoke with the
neurologist who examined her brain scans after her most recent
fall. She had a subdural hematoma, blood on the brain. It would
most certainly kill her if they didn't operate and relieve the
pressure. But at her age the chances of surviving an intensive
surgery like that weren't great. And she didn't want any heroic
measures. She wanted to die. She finally got her wish. It broke
my heart, but this was a gift I could help give her. Peace. I told
the doctor that we wouldn't be doing any operation. I sobbed
and sobbed.

That last week with my grandma, in the nursing home, I
thought a lot about her life. They said she didn't have long and
I refused to leave her side. My brothers and I took shifts. No
one should have to die alone. Especially not a woman that had
been left alone, been lonely for so much of her life, and yet had
accomplished so much and loved me so well. Her frail body
breathing quietly in the bed, the morphine coursing through
her veins as the blood on her brain pressed towards its final
purpose. She had a dignified air about her nonetheless. Her eyes
closed, those sharp brown eyes, the ones I see when I look in

the mirror, the ones I see when I look at my daughter, the ones that I will never see again and yet see every day. We are flesh and blood. I would not be if she was not. She and I, both depressives, had both toyed with Hamlet's immortal question. But at this moment, the question was not "to be or not to be." It was only a question of when. Now we had to wait and let time take its course. It wouldn't be long now. She hung on until my mom flew in from the other coast. We stood in a circle around her and sang her off to the angels. It was beautiful.

Most knew her as ████████. I called her Grandma. My daughter called her Gammy. My mom called her Mom. I found out only in the last year of her life that she was born as Dorothy, but hated the name and dropped it as soon as she could. Having the name Dorothy close to when *The Wizard of Oz* was a hit movie must not have been much different than my friend Ariel who was in elementary school when *The Little Mermaid* came out. Kids can be cruel. No one ever picked on my name, but I got plenty of shit for having red hair, so I can relate.

Grandma wrote a memoir in the last years of her life. It may have started after she got out of the mental hospital, I'm not sure. It gave her purpose again. We helped her get a laptop, and she would regularly call me when it acted up. My limited tech skills usually sufficed - a restart here, unplugging a cord there: basic knowledge for an elder Millennial like me that was totally mysterious to one from the Greatest Generation. She refused to get the internet, because of all the bad things she had heard about it on cable news. She sent me long lists of movies to add to her Netflix list. That was when DVDs from Netflix came in those red and white envelopes. She was amazed that after I typed her list into the computer, the DVDs arrived in her mailbox a few days later. She complained that she had once written them a letter and never heard back. I chuckled. You can't mail a letter to a tech company, can you?

Ever the researcher, the seasoned Washington, DC journalist, she would call me with questions to "look up on that internet." It was magical to her but she didn't want to get too close. I was happy to act the hero when it was really Google that was surfacing the facts. I was merely a courier between the information superhighway and the country road my grandma lived on, translating digital to analog.

My grandmother grew up in the Great Depression. She was born in 1929 on the kitchen table of a farmhouse in Oklahoma. Her 15-year-old mother had been raped in a barn by a much older man and then forced by her father to marry him. I have no doubt this was the very definition of a shotgun wedding. My great-grandmother had considered suicide when she found out she was pregnant, but as she were to tell it years later, and my grandma recounted in her memoir, an angel appeared in the rafters of the barn and told her that her child would do good in the world and that she must live to raise her. She had planned to hang herself in the rafters of that barn, but she turned and walked back into the farmhouse. She married and took her rapist's name. She labored and bled in the kitchen until her baby girl came into the world.

The marriage didn't last long. They moved a lot, my great-grandmother and her daughter. My great-grandmother worked as a waitress and enjoyed the company of the bottle and the men that accompanied it. My grandmother describes nights where she was left in a small apartment alone while her mother was working late and partying later. She was a toddler. I had heard the story before, but when I most recently read these words in her memoir, a profound sorrow and pain gripped my heart. I have a toddler. She will be three next month. She is beautiful, spirited, and feisty. We never leave her alone. Sometimes we leave her in the care of trusted others, usually paying the high price for trust, but never alone. Toddlers are happy a lot and can sometimes entertain themselves, but also cry a lot and need constant attention and reassurance.

They need to be held. Children need to be constantly held. They are able to play so independently because they know a caring adult is near to pick them up if they fall. I imagine my little grandma, not more than three, looking mournfully out the window, coloring alone, or rummaging through the cupboards for food. It makes me sad. This story was why I refused to let her be alone in her final days and hours.

This isolation, this neglect, was this the genesis of her depression, her chronic mental illness - or was it there, her genetic destiny, before she even appeared on that kitchen table in Oklahoma?

Her mother married and divorced again and again. Eventually they ended up in California. It was the Great Depression, which hit hard in the dust bowl of Oklahoma. They dreamed of a better, more prosperous life. They hitched a ride with a car dealer who needed to deliver a Cadillac to San Francisco. Her mother convinced him that she'd marry him when they got there, but when they arrived the girls ducked out at the first glimpse of the Pacific Ocean. They started a new life. Grandma reported good memories from that time: a good student with social graces, she made friends and sang on the radio.

Later, as a young woman, she met a young sailor who was shipping off to war. World War II was raging in the Pacific and the boys were shipping out. Both gifted writers, they exchanged letters. They devised a code so that she would know his whereabouts. Sailors were not allowed to share their locations, lest the enemy might intercept the mail, so they made a plan. They made a list of the hit songs of the day and matched it to areas in the Pacific where the Navy was active. "Boogie Woogie Bugle Boy" was Iwo Jima. "I'll Be Home for Christmas" was Pearl Harbor. Frank Sinatra and others provided their depression-era GPS.

When the handsome sailor returned, they married. ███████ ███████ had sparkly blue eyes and a prominent chin. His first name was ███████ but everyone called him ███. That's right, ███ ███████: you can't get a more generic American man's name than that. His grandparents had been named ███████. I wonder if a fellow named ███████ ███████ would have done as well as ███ ███ did. His handsome charm and quick wits served him well. Especially with my glamorous, intelligent grandmother on his arm. They went to college together. He cashed in his GI Bill. He graduated but she didn't, withdrawing to follow him to Washington, DC to start his career as a journalist. She had a career as a journalist too, writing for newspapers, later working as a press secretary for a prominent senator from Oregon. Their baby █████, my mother, came along soon enough. A red-headed beauty in her own right.

After 20 years, ███ and ████████ divorced. He remarried. She never did. Her depressions were dark and long and not responsive to treatment. He couldn't take it anymore. He had a new family now, having married a woman with three children. My mother bounced between them but mostly stayed with her mother. There is more in the memoir, but it is hard to pick it up. Interesting stories about tea with Jackie Kennedy devolve into her feelings of betrayal by my grandfather or her mother or needless details trying to capture everything left in her memory from that time. There are also painful stories of loneliness and depression, and it is too much for me to process.

My grandpa wrote a memoir too. His 13th publication, it is for sale on Amazon and has had modest sales. There are only four copies of Grandma's memoir—three are on my bookshelf and one is on my mom's. She lived on a fixed income and had to report her assets to the county every year to qualify for her public housing. Grandpa died well-off in a big house in a nice neighborhood. She was afraid someone would find out about her book, because she knew it was so valuable. Poor people aren't allowed to have anything valuable if they want government help. She mailed copy after copy to publishers around the country, sometimes getting a kind rejection notice, usually getting nothing. She was sure that when the right person read it she would be well-compensated—but she would put it in my name because she didn't want to lose her little apartment. We self-published and presented it to her on her 90th birthday. She complained that we had changed her title from *What's Lack of Love Got to Do With It? Everything* to *Love is Everything*. The negative (unconscious?) mangling of the iconic Tina Turner classic was too much for my wife and me to put on the cover. We took creative editorial license, with the title only. We were the publishers, after all. But that was Grandma, a pain in the ass. Sharp and critical and opinionated and amazing to the end.

I loved my grandma. We used to drive in her old Mustang along the coast, winding the back roads of our rural county. The winds from the ocean blew salty air through the strait, through the car windows when I cranked them down. Grandma liked to look for eagles and we often found them. She talked about a spiritual connection. I had thought they were really awesome since I wrote a report about them in 5th grade. Now, whenever I visit that magical place, I look for eagles. When one flies overhead I always think of her.

The day after I left the day hospital I went for a hike with friends. An eagle flew overhead and I knew it was her spirit greeting me. I suppose that is my spirituality. Connection to the afterlife. I'm glad she is still in my heart; she deserves to be in heaven and I would take the wheel and drive her there if I could. Eagles usually fly alone, but with a calm, wise presence that represents freedom across our land. I truly hope she is free. I know she is.

Bloodline

Did I inherit my depression from my grandmother? Is it a genetic defect, or did all those tough years change her, shape a personality that shaped a personality that shaped my personality? She raised my mother and my mother raised me.

The field of epigenetics fascinates me. There is evidence that we can inherit the trauma of our ancestors. Experiences in the environment change the body, change the brain, shape the lives of future generations. This phenomenon is most apparent in the experiences of the Native American people. The Cherokee people, from my grandma's native Oklahoma, were marched in the Trail of Tears from their home to a reservation hundreds of miles from where their ancestors had lived for generations.

While the Cherokee and many other tribes have displayed great resilience and amazingly kept their culture and customs alive, despite this attempted cultural genocide, they have also struggled with the legacy of severe trauma. There is a generational cycle of poverty, alcoholism, drug addiction, and other challenges that are pervasive for people of Native American descent. There was always a rumor of Cherokee blood in our family. I was supposedly 1/8th Native. However, a recent take-home genetics test placed my ancestry squarely on the other side of the Atlantic.

The egg that became my mother was inside my *in utero* grandmother's womb when she was in my great-grandmother's womb. My mother was there on that kitchen table in Oklahoma. Not even the size of a pea, she came into the world the product of rape and shame and pain. The table was set. Many years later when I struggle with intractable emotional pain, I wonder how much of this story, the experiences of these women, are as part of my body as they were theirs? Did I even have a chance when depression was my inheritance? Genetics lying in wait for that vulnerable moment in my life when they switched on and expressed themselves, burying my stable life with the colossal weight of my grandmother's trauma and loneliness. What have my daughters inherited from me? I have more questions than I have answers. And then there was this father I never really knew—what genetic inheritance came from him?

Biological Father

The day I first learned the name of my biological father is crystal clear in my memory. I call him biological because he was never my father, until that day anyway. I was raised by another man I called Dad. I had that man's last name. "███████." I have always been and always will be ███ ██████. But I had a mysterious second middle name on my birth certificate. I didn't even know about it until I was seven years old. I knew that ████ was my middle name, but one day my mom showed me my birth certificate and pointed out that I was special—that I had two middle names. ██████ ██████ ██████ is my full name. My brothers thought it was funny; I thought it was interesting, but shrugged it off and went back to playing with GI Joes and firecrackers.

I know for sure that I was seven then, as hazy as childhood memories are, because I have a distinct memory of my eighth birthday. My mom picked me up from my elementary school as usual. We lived in a nice neighborhood in the city. We walked home along tree-lined streets. It was a mild June day—perfect weather, really. My mom seemed nervous, uncharacteristically quiet for my usually chatty mother, especially on a sunny day. And then, a few blocks from home, she came out with it. "I have something to talk with you about, son." She said it in an oddly formal way, almost like a script that she had worked out and now had to stick to. "Ummm.... ok", I said, my floppy red head nodding as the sun bounced off my highlights. I stared at the ground, not sure what was coming, but pretty sure I was in trouble for something. "Remember how I told you about your second middle name?" She looked pleadingly into my eyes. "Ummm yeah... ███, right?" "Yes...well, that isn't actually a middle name... I mean it is your middle name... but you have it because it is someone else's last name." I was confused. What the heck was she talking about? ███ was clearly a first name. I had a kid in my class named ███. I was confused. "What do you mean?" I asked with a curious look on my face. "Well, when you were born 8 years ago...I, ummm...well...before that... before your Dad and I were married... there was another man named ██ ███████ that I knew." I was really confused now.

My eight-year-old self must have heard of the birds and the bees and sex and how babies are made and all that, but it was still abstract and certainly not a concept that had the potential to tear apart one's entire identity, especially at such a vulnerable age. "Remember the wedding pictures I showed you where I was in the white dress and I said I was pregnant with you?" "Ummm yeah...the ones with all the rainbows when dad had a big beard?" It was the eighties by then, but my parents were still hippies. "Yeah." She gulped. I could tell we were getting to the punchline, the big reveal about what I had done wrong and what my punishment would be, but I couldn't figure out what that had to do with rainbows and middle names and the early eighties. "Well, about Dad—he will always be your dad, but ███ ████, the one I knew before I married your dad…he is your biological father." This hit me like a ton of bricks, as if they were falling from all directions.

I can only imagine now how much she must have thought about when to tell me this secret, how hard it must have been to keep. Who she must have consulted. When do you deliver this news to a kid? Some adopted kids are never told until an inebriated uncle or jealous sibling lets it slip, while some grow up always knowing that biology is not what connects them to the parents that are raising them. But this was extra weird because my mom was still my mom, but my dad…who was he to me now? It seemed that I had two fathers…or maybe only one was real? But which one?

I have an eight-year old daughter now. I see how in so many ways she is embracing her independent identity lately—much of which comes from the unwavering acceptance and belief that I am her father and always have been, that her sister is 100% her sister, and that her mom has always told her the truth about who she is. I can't imagine holding on to such a secret and what it would do to the girl whose brown eyes are the same as those of that little boy standing frozen on the sidewalk.

My mother and I walked in silence for a while. She could tell I needed to process what I had just heard. I would get the full story later, a brief love affair that reached from coast to coast, but today I was more concerned with where this left me—how I fit into our family now. I was different. I had two little brothers, once full, now half, and an older brother—once half, now step. Dad called us the red riot: wild boys connected by blood and fire. What happened now that my blood wasn't the same as theirs? "Who am I now?" I thought. In later years I would spend time with this long-lost biological father of mine, but from an early age my identity was shaken and fragile.

Reverend Father

I was 20, maybe 19. Certainly not old enough to go into a bar, but old enough to be out in the world alone for long periods of time. The time had come. I had been doing a lot of soul searching. I had exhausted the naive idea that if I went off to college I would soon achieve the American Dream and everything would be ok. I was still limping away from my first major depressive episode, my first dance with medication, my first suicide attempt, the first time I dropped out of college. It was a list of firsts that I was determined to be lasts. I just needed to figure out who I was and what I wanted to do and be and everything would be ok and none of those painful things would happen again. But they did, there was a second time for all of that. The depression always comes back and wrecks me.

But this time I knew that meeting my "real" father was a key part of unlocking my identity and my destiny, of re-opening a door that I had kept locked for many years.

His name was on my birth certificate; though buried as a second middle name, it was there nonetheless. And I knew very little about him, beyond the few recollections that my mom shared. I did meet him once as a child. I was 8 or 9, around my daughter's current age. My grandfather lived in a beach town on the east coast, where we had visited before. It was a place full of happy memories, where my brothers and I swam in the ocean, where Grandpa made pancakes in the morning and taught us to play pool in the afternoon. But another person lived in that town too, a mystery man that it turned out held a secret about me that I was just learning of.

We met him at a diner. I remember there were pastrami sandwiches and pickles on the menu and lots of color on the walls. It was a cloudy day. My insides felt drained of life, as the sky was drained of color. I was terrified. My parents were divorcing. My dad wasn't really my dad and I was about to meet the man who was. We had round-trip tickets from the west coast. We weren't planning to stay, only to say hello and do what there is never a right time to do: reunite a child with the parent they never knew. The one they escaped from.

He was old, in his 70s; around my grandfather's age, but they had nothing else in common. My grandfather had a well-kept white beard, the dignified look of a retired journalist turned novelist. My biological father's beard and hair were long and gray and scraggly, the undignified look of an unrenounced hippie. He wore a dirty raincoat and shorts revealing knobby knees attached to tanned legs tucked into well-worn, formerly white, now-gray sneakers. He carried a weathered backpack with a blue bike helmet snapped through the handle. He smiled and his deep-set eyes went deeper, crinkly eyes that almost disappeared behind a broad smile. He had my eyes, or rather, I had his. I had inherited my grandmother's piercing brown irises, but the brows, the cheekbones, the frame of these windows into my soul, they were his.

He hugged my mother; always the graceful and warm socialite, she introduced me as ▮▮▮▮ and he as ▮. I was frozen in place. I'm not sure if I hugged him or shook his hand but my elbows most certainly didn't move far from my sides. He looked like the homeless men that I had seen when we went into the city, the ones that begged for change in the streets and talked to themselves on corners.

He was very nice, with a warm southern drawl, but I don't remember any of what was said. I just remember being terrified that this true part of me, the part of me that had just been revealed, was a homeless man who lived in a tent in his friend's backyard. After we finished eating, he stepped away to go to the bathroom, as we did a few minutes later. Being young I went into the ladies room with my mother. When we returned he looked scared, as if we had left him again, abruptly and without notice, as my mother had when she was pregnant with me. Relief washed over his wrinkled brow.

He made a show of paying the check with cash. We got a picture

of me and him outside of the restaurant. My mom had brought
one of those disposable cameras that were all the rage in the late
eighties. We went to a shop and he bought me a leather fanny
pack. To this day I think that is the only gift he ever gave me,
besides my life and my genetics. I didn't see him again until I
was an adult and could do it on my own terms. I had so many
questions that were to be tucked away for a decade. Who was
this homeless man that my mother had once loved, and why
was he my father?

██████ █████ █████, III was born and bred in the South.
From a family of bankers and confederate generals and presidential aides, his father was a tire salesman and his mother
stayed home to raise him and his brother. Their childhood was
interrupted during several long periods where their mother was
committed to the asylum and they were farmed out to live with
extended family. I have never definitively heard why she was in
the hospital, but from what I gather it was severe and unrelenting depression.

When █ grew up, he dreamed of being a preacher. After seminary he became an ordained Southern Baptist minister. He married and had four lovely daughters. He led a congregation in
Alabama. From the pictures I've seen of the time, it was a good
American life—on the surface anyway. The civil rights movement was in full swing and he took the side of his black neighbors, not a popular position in his circles. Four little girls died
in a church explosion not far from his own church, touching the
lives of people he had grown close to, touching him deeply and
painfully. He became disillusioned and eventually left his post
at the church.

My sisters, who I met years later, have shared and written
stories about that time. He worked as a paramedic and as a
chaplain in a mental hospital and they spent time in communes.
He would leave for months at a time and then come home
and crawl into a sleeping bag and sleep for weeks. He would
beat their mother. And then one day he finally left for good. A
few years later they heard he was having a baby with a much

younger woman. He was in his fifties by then, she was 26. His eldest daughter at that time was 28.

He got together with my mother in his middle age, but the families had history that went back a generation. My grandfather's second wife's father had been a seminary professor. One of his brightest students had been my ██ ██████. ██████ and █ had grown up as friends.

My mother had been living in California and engaged to ████ ██████, but they broke up and she went to the other coast to study massage. Her family had been interested in new-age thought and there was a place called the ████████████████ ████████████████████ that was based on ████████████ ████████████████████. My mom studied at the massage school there. My grandfather was the editor-in-chief for their membership magazine, ████████████████. It also had a library full of texts on spirituality. ██ ██████, by then an unmoored hippie emerging from the seventies, liked to hang out there.

He was much older and seemingly wise and full of knowledge and she was young and beautiful and full of curiosity and thirsty for truth. It was a whirlwind affair that quickly went cold, and she began to miss her friends and her life in California. As interesting as he was, he was not interested in working, or making a home, or being a functional adult. She wanted a family. He followed her across the country. She became pregnant and he found work as a dishwasher. He refused to get any other type of job. At night, as her belly grew in their small apartment, he would sermonize. Once he began talking it went on for hours, manic-lecturing on religion and truth. She became scared for her life and her baby, not that he would physically hurt her, but the harm that might come from trying to make a life, a home with this man. She didn't know what his wife and children had endured, but she sensed it.

I can only imagine how terrifying this must have been for her. In my experience, pregnancy is terrifying enough when everything else in your life is relatively stable. One day when he was out at his dishwashing job, she called a friend and confided her fears and her situation. Her friend called her ex-fiance, still a dear friend, who came and picked her up in Santa Cruz and brought her back to San Jose. The story goes that he had a dream about helping a boat into shore and she dreamed of him in a house full of quilts.

He picked her up in his old Volkswagen and they rented a fancy hotel room off the freeway. It was rumored to be the honeymoon suite, with a heart-shaped red bathtub. They still very much loved each other and had had a long past relationship. Getting back together wasn't so crazy. Except for the other man's baby in her belly.

He proposed marriage that night in the motel room with the heart-shaped bathtub. He didn't care that she was pregnant. He loved her. He would be the father. He wanted to be the father. He had had a dream, and in their still idealistic generation, dreams held the weight of truth.

They married in February. He wore white tails and she a white dress, big with child. There were rainbows all around. I wonder how many people knew that he wasn't really the father. I was born at a birth home near a hospital. A professional photographer friend of theirs documented the occasion. The scene was dim, with lit-up smiling faces. There was water involved. Everyone seemed to be naked, well, my mom certainly was, and my dad shirtless. My older brother was standing around looking wide-eyed. He had clothes on at least. In my personal experience, witnessing a birth is terrifying enough for a grown man; I can only imagine the experience of a nine-year-old boy.

A friend was once visiting my house in high school. I was in the bathroom and she started paging through a photo album that was on the coffee table. I think it was June and my mom enjoyed looking through them to remember my birthday. I came back in the room and was immediately mortified. I grabbed the book out of her hands and put it on the shelf. Fucking hippies. Everyone had clothes on when my kids were born. But looking back, as normal as I pretend to be, that was just the right way for me to come into the world, with these people, in that place. There was a lot of love in that house.

I grew up with three brothers. The most noticeable feature - for all of us - is our bright red hair. People tend to notice that first, that and our rambunctious energy. We are definitely brothers. A swirl of fire, the red riot lives up to our reputation. But, as soon as I knew I was different, it perpetually gnawed at me.

████ ████ ████ is listed under "Father" on my birth certificate, right below my full name, ████ ████ ████ ████. The only hint of ██ is hidden in my second middle name. It turned out that ████ was the real father after all. He earned it. I struggled with this for years, but now it is clear. One man gave me my eyes and the other gave me my life.

It wasn't until later, when I met my older sisters and looked through family albums, that I found a father that resembled me. As my brothers and I grew into men, their features resembled our dad's…the Sicilian nose, the wide smile, the piercing blue eyes. My deep brown eyes, square chin, and long legs with knobby knees set me apart.

That old homeless man in the deli had looked nothing like the clean-cut man I was turning into. And then, a few pages into the album, I saw it. It was a picture of me. But no—it wasn't me. It was him, at my age. Copper hair, deep-set dark eyes, and a square jaw. Handsome and full of youth. I slipped the photo out of the album and ran to the mirror. I held it up next to my face.

The resemblance was indisputable. Whatever doubts I had about this strange story that my parents had told me, vanished. This man was my father. I excitedly got my sister and showed her what I had discovered, what she and her sisters had seen the moment I walked into their lives at 19. The man that had raised them had long ago been replaced by a scraggly old man, but here was his mirror image, standing in her kitchen.

Later, on that trip, my sister told me more about him...stories she later put in her own memoir. I could tell she was nervous, being careful with her words. We drank tea in her kitchen. She told me about the abuse, the nights of terror that she and our sister endured while he shouted and laid hands on her mother. The cult-like adherence to commune life, the rejection of any hint of modernity, a toxic dose of the lighter hippie worldview that I grew up steeped in.

A period that began with a deeper connection to my identity ended with more questions. These deep-set dark eyes, this disarming handsome smile—was it just the wrapping of a monster lying in wait? He was never formally diagnosed, but my sisters are sure that he was manic-depressive, severely bipolar. My still-fragile mind, in recovery from my first significant breakdown, was terrified that the man in those pictures and I had more in common than I wanted to accept. The later pictures, him dressed in church clothes surrounded by his pretty wife and darling daughters, look not unlike the pictures of me and my family at a recent wedding. My daughters aren't living in a home with secrets of violence and rage. But I still carry a fear that this trait lays in wait deep within me.

As I write this down, connections are being made. Stories that have rattled around in my head for years—it's something different to get them out and down on the page. Is this part of why I have so diligently stayed connected to psychiatric care? Many people with my condition have periods where they abandon conventional treatment entirely, only to come back into care in extreme crisis. I am terrified of the monster inside of me, a manic-depressive demon that has never fully seen the light of day. If I hadn't been on one mood stabilizer or another since before I could buy beer, would I be far beyond the bad side of crazy? I am restless, I long for travel, I have periods of irritability where my wife and I argue and doors are slammed. I've never struck her, screamed or called her names, or scared my children with my rage.

My children love to play the "scary monster" game with me. I act big and hulking and silly and scary. The key is to be a little scary but not too scary. Sometimes my eyes grow too wide or I roar too loud or I wrestle them too hard and they cry and we stop, and then before long they smile and ask for "more scary monster, DADDY!" With girls, especially, I want them to learn that when they say "stop," that is what a man is supposed to do. Their words are powerful and I respect them.

My house is full of giggling and laughter and tears and joy. When I am in really bad shape I disappear into my mind, into my phone, into the TV. I'm not present. They try to engage me but I withdraw. They beg for the scary monster to come out and play, but he turns away. I hope and pray that whether it is me, or any other scary monsters my daughters meet, that when they say stop their words are heeded. I am their protector, but I can't always be there. In my life to date, with no history of violence, I am no longer afraid of what harm I might do. I'm more afraid of what I might not do. More specifically, that I might have a breakdown and not be there to hold them when they cry and hear their laughter when they play. I want to be there.

I spent time with ▇ when I was a young man in my twenties. It was always a bit strange and confusing but I knew it was important. What I am most grateful for, out of this whole weird story, is that his daughters have adopted me. He may not have been my father, but they are definitely my sisters. We have an amazing connection, and the same deep-set crinkly eyes, and we laugh and laugh and laugh. We are definitely related. Genetic inheritance is an interesting thing. Would I give my sisters back if I could delete ▇ from my birth certificate and my DNA, delete the bipolar gene, delete this whole weird story? Never. I can't imagine my life without them. As for the bipolar, I suppose it has been responsible for quite a ride. These ancestors gave me life and I am grateful for it.

5

Dad

"My father wasn't around..." — *Hamilton*

The *Hamilton* soundtrack is in heavy rotation in our car. The show is amazing. I am in the mood for some American history on the way to school dropoff that day, I guess. Or maybe I'm a little hypomanic. "Siri, play 'Dear Theodosia'," I say in the general direction of the phone in my pocket. Magically the song starts playing through the van's speakers.

This morning, as the gentle tune of this sweet song begins to play, I look in the rear-view mirror and see a set of familiar eyes. Deep-set, brown, intense, curious. My grandmother's eyes. My biological father's eyes. My eyes. She gazes forward, half asleep or maybe a little sad, it is hard to tell with her sometimes. But I see her lips moving. She knows all the words to this song.

My first-born. She is beautiful. I wonder how my depressions have affected her, even the not-so-major ones. Depression has been present in her home at various periods of her childhood. Our marital struggles, my tendency to withdraw at the first sign of conflict, when my wife comes home in a bad mood, probably just tired and needing to vent, but I can't handle any more human misery today. My job fills me to the brim.

Maple Bars

When I was five my dad broke the kitchen door. I don't know what I did. He was so mad at me. I was in the yard with him and he started yelling at me. I was good at pissing him off. I scampered into the house with him hot on my heels. I ran into my mother's arms and she held me close. He glared and slammed the door behind him, shattering the glass window. I buried my tears in my mom's bosom. I don't remember ever seeing him angry like that again. Something changed. He started taking me to donuts on the way to first grade. Something softened between us. He wasn't angry with me so much. My behavior improved.

I wonder if he felt trapped, in his late thirties at that point. I know that feeling now. I totally get it. He was responsible for four boys. Mouths to feed. His business failing. Did he look at me and regret taking me in? Putting his name on my birth certificate when I wasn't really his? More responsibility than he could bear, one more inspired moment in youth leading to long-term burden in later adulthood?

But something changed. We ate maple bars and he asked me about school. He told me about his job running the telemarketing company, the race car they had sponsored, his past career running city council races, saving enough money so we could move north and build a house in the woods. We had later moved to the city because his commute was too long. The house in the woods had been his dream since touring the country in a VW bus with my older brother, staying at communes, dreaming of a family life free of the modern struggles he faced in the big city.

Race cars sounded cool to me. He didn't tell me that it was bankrupting the company. Maybe he didn't realize it yet. Maybe he knew my mom was planning to tell me about ▪. He wanted a shot at being my father, my real father, because he knew the man waiting for me in a tent in that beach town on the other coast couldn't be the man I needed in my life. He was right.

I want to connect more intentionally with my older daughter. She is older now, as am I. We are both hitting a new developmental stage. She is pushing fast beyond eight, me hanging on tight to 38. She is active and we've been playing ball and just set up ping pong on the picnic table outside. She is fascinated by my writing, always checking my word count. She has started to accept my offers to run errands and ride bikes. I love her. I remember the tears in my eyes when I held her for the first time. It had been a long night of labor but they connected the epidural and we were able to rest. My wife started to push again and I held her hand. And then we heard a cry and before long this sweet creature was clinging to her mama's bare skin. She was so familiar, had been with us for almost a year. Longer in our hopes and dreams. She was just on the outside now. Skin to skin is what is recommended now—I guess the hippies got something right. As they stitched my wife up the doctor handed our new baby to me. I held her to my bare chest. Tears of joy ran down my cheeks. "Thank you," I choked out as she purred and I melted, our hearts beating in unison. Life is amazing.

I'm not leaving. As many times as I've thought about it after a stressful incident at home, I never have packed a bag, left for a pack of cigarettes and never came back, like a client once described his father's departure. I don't smoke, so I guess that's out. But Paul Simon has 50 other ways if I'm looking for a way to leave. I'm staying. My parents both married and divorced three times. I'd like my kids to tell a different story.

I know bits and pieces of the story of why my parents divorced. My uncle recently came out with it. "Your dad was transgendered." I assured him I already knew, but I understood why he would think I might not. It was a family secret. A Catholic family's secret. He had been at seminary as a boy and they found dresses in his closet and panties hidden in his dresser. His parents were summoned and he was disciplined—brutally I imagine. I might have to call Child Protective Services if I heard about it now, but it was the fifties. It was never talked about again.

I remember the day we left my dad. I was devastated the day they told us about the divorce. Sitting outside the house in the woods on a picnic table. My heart ripped in two and I was silent. He was my father, but not really, and now we were leaving him. His "gender identity crisis" was too much for her. She didn't think it was healthy for her boys to be around. I didn't really understand it, but honestly I didn't think it was that weird. Certainly not enough to break up a family over. We left him in the house in the woods and moved to a rental on the other side of town.

He put his gender issues back in the closet. He lived as a man. He was a he. He remarried. Weekends at their house were stricter, more rules, more cleaning, more chores. Mom's house was like *Lord of the Flies* in comparison.

Memory Loss

In my most recent round of depression I considered ECT. Yes, *One Flew Over the Cuckoo's Nest*-style electroconvulsive "shock" therapy. The doctors say it has come a long way since Jack Nicholson's iconic scene under the care of Nurse Ratched. My psychiatrist suggested that it could be our last ditch option. So did my boss. He is a psychiatrist too. It is safer now, they insist. They finally got the voltage right, I guess. I made an intake appointment. Two months out was as soon as I could get in. Last ditch. This option felt beyond nuclear. I've heard that the worst part is the memory loss. I spoke to a woman that had no memory of her sister's wedding. But it also cured her devastating depression.

I don't want to lose my memories, this precious time with my children. Even the hard ones. The screaming and the tantrums and the stress. I want to remember it all. Maybe that is why I'm writing this, logging memories in case my brain needs an ECT reboot someday and I forget.

Especially my memories of my father, the dad that raised me. They are precious to me. His is the name on my birth certificate. When he put his dresses back into the closet in the mid-nineties, he changed his name to the more androgenous ███. He kept his pronouns and his dry-cleaned shirts and khaki pants. But it was a nod to the woman that was beneath the surface, a hint of expression, in an otherwise unsuspiciously masculine man.

Family Secret

I am now curious what happened that led to his need to come out. He was a family man with a good job. He was making it in the world of men. But then he lost his business and he was in that house in the woods full of boys, going to therapy, and trying to piece together who he was. Almost 40, like I am now. I only now understand the amount of pressure he was under. The dresses were still in the closet in his soul. He had a big house now, with lots of closets, and the only one strong enough to beat him down was himself. He bought some dresses. He also bought an androgynous stuffed bear he named ███, the same name he later gave himself. I don't know how the discussion went with my mother, but he started wearing the dresses around the house. He didn't wear makeup or anything, just these big shapeless cotton dresses. They weren't even that feminine, no flowers, more like a tunic or a robe. A look totally masculine in the Middle East probably. But this was America. Men wear pants here.

We didn't have neighbors that could see in, we were in the woods. We were the only witnesses. He had a job now in the city and put on a pressed shirt and colorful tie every week day. He was an administrator at a small private college. He liked the job. I think he even shared with his boss that he was thinking about a gender change. They were supportive. But my mom wasn't. It was too much for her. These little boys needed a father, a real father, not a transgendered person, woman, whatever he was now. He seemed to be moving forward with the transition. We left. I didn't really know why. I just remember liking holding ███████ the bear. He was a comfort when I heard my parents fighting in the other room. How could such a nice creature cause so much trouble, break up my family?

I was super confused now. Not only was my father not my father, but he might soon not even be a man? But that didn't come to pass. He put the dresses back in the closet, he married a woman that loved his brilliant mind and his innate masculinity. The college grew into a university and he became a vice president. He later took jobs in California and New Jersey that paid him very well, topped up a retirement account devastated by child support and divorce settlements. But he stayed in that house in the woods until my youngest brother finished high school. ████████ ████████ the man got along in the world great. He was successful. My mom gets a big social security check every month because of the high income he commanded.

But what if he had gone through with it? What if he had become ████████ ████████, the transgender woman? What if he didn't quite pass and people suspected what might be between his legs? Or he did pass and he faced the discrimination of a woman in a man's world? This was long before Caitlyn Jenner was on the cover of *Sports Illustrated* or we had a female presidential nominee. Progress was being made in gender equality and LGBTQ rights, but it was a very different time. I wonder how many other fathers had dresses in their closet? How many still do?

The lesson I learned from him, however dysfunctional, was that you need to set aside who you are, deep down, if you want to survive in this world. If you want to raise a family, if you want your kids to be healthy and strong and self-sustaining, maybe even affluent, inconvenient secrets must be buried. A man's worth is built on the image he projects, the identity he shows the world, so it should be carefully curated. And as strangely fake as it must have seemed he would have to be, he was one of the most authentic human beings I have ever known. ███ was a lovely person. He answered to "Dad" for me and my brothers.

A few years ago Dad called and told me that he had rented an apartment near the university, one of those pod-like tiny ones. For foreign college students and men going through divorce, I had heard. He was leaving my stepmother for the second time. He spared me the details but I understood. All of his boys were grown now. I think there was an itch for freedom inside of him. I talked to him at the park about it, his only grandchild playing nearby. ███ loved her Papa. He had just returned from the world cup in Brazil, an epic trip with my older brother. He told me more about the apartment. I pictured the neighborhood it was in. I had gone to graduate school nearby. I was happy that he would be living just a few miles from us. It made me really happy. I always felt better when he was near.

The next week I was at work, preparing for an interview with a potential new recruit. I was the director and my presence was necessary. My stepmom called and asked me if I had heard from my dad. They were separating but still close, he came to the house several days a week still. She hadn't heard from him in three days. His work had called. She was his emergency contact. He had missed some important meetings. That wasn't like him. I had called him and left him a message a few days before. It wasn't uncommon for him to take a few days to get back to me, but he hadn't called.

She asked me to call the local hospitals. I did. What a weird thing to have to do. No one by that name. I remembered what he had told me about the apartment. I didn't remember the name of it, but how many pod apartments could be in that neighborhood? It turns out there were a few. I finally got through to an apartment manager that recognized his name. When I explained the situation she offered to call the maintenance man who could check the apartment. He was an hour out. My wife met up with my stepmother and they went to the address I gave them and waited for the maintenance man. I went into my interview. Totally distracted. Halfway in my wife texted me. "You better come, right now." I knew. I left in a hurry.

I was holding my breath, driving in an invisible fog. My wife met me half a block away. She hugged me. We came upon my stepmother sobbing—wailing—outside the apartment building. The fire department was there, the police arrived. The maintenance man looked shook up and told me what he had found. The tenant of his apartment was dead. After the police had surveyed the scene and concluded there was no foul play, they let us go up into the apartment. He had a heart condition, it was a four story walk up. There was an explanation. But to me there could be no explanation for why my sweet Dad, my real father, had to die at 63. My stepmother came out with tear-stained cheeks. I went in alone. He lay on his back on the floor of the small apartment. His skin was tinted blue gray. It had been a few days. ███ was dead. I said goodbye.

The policemen had opened the window. It was a cool sunny day. I stood and looked out onto the view of the ship canal, imagining his spirit floating out to sea. As I turned to leave, I noticed a rack with clothes hanging on it. There were several shapeless cotton dresses blowing in the breeze. They had flowers on them. "Goodbye, Dad," I said to his lifeless corpse, a beautiful shell of the person who had loved me so well.

One of the traumatic things about being first on the scene to someone's death, to confirming they are dead, without a doubt it is him, his body identified on the floor, that you have to call the people that love him and break their hearts. There were a lot of phone calls. Each call began with the news, then a gasp and a long sob. As I write this I pull my hands from the keyboard and sob audibly into them. It was so painful. My heart was breaking. I called my older brother in California. He got on a plane. I called my younger brother overseas. I called my dad's brother and asked him to call all of their siblings. That was a lot of calls.

I also asked my uncle to come to be with us. He looked just like my dad and I had grown close to him when I lived near him in college. His kids were grown. He was available. We needed a dad around. We were a mess. He came right away. I drove to my hometown to tell my brother in person.

The memorial packed over 200 people into the chapel. Business colleagues and dear friends, many were both. With some of them he had been open about his gender struggles, it was an open secret for him I think. But it wasn't advertised on his resume. He was the best man at my wedding and the best man in my life. I am so lucky that he followed his dream and loved me as his own. He was an amazing human.

I miss him. I am sorry that he doesn't get to see my girls grow up. He would have been an amazing grandfather. He was for a few years anyway. My feelings about the afterlife are unsettled but sometimes I like to imagine that my youngest daughter is my dad reincarnated. She is a ball of love and energy and femininity. There is no doubt that she is a girl. She tells me all the time. She loves tutus and unicorns and dollies. She owns lots of dresses with flowers on them. She will be a beautiful woman. I want to give her a really good life. I want to give her the best life. I will never beat her, never tell her she can't be who she is. I will love whoever she brings home. If she someday tells me she is a he, I will hug him and love him and call him whatever name he, or they, wants. I am a bit lost with all these girls around anyway.

But I have a feeling she will always be my ███, the girl with the unicorn crown, the unicorn tights, the unicorn boots. Just like he was my ███. My unicorn, my savior. My father. I miss him. I am sobbing as I write this, but I can't stop writing. I need to get this out, this pain, this love. I never want to forget him. I want to stay healthy and avoid ECT and keep my memories, even the ones where my heart was ripped in half but I was still alive. I am still alive. I miss you, Dad.

6

Travel Therapy

Esalen

After the incident in the bathtub I tried to go back to school, but it didn't last long. The depression was lifting, in fits and starts, but I couldn't stay. I entertained the idea of traveling. I'd been to Canada, but never south of the border. Never beyond California, the state of my birth. I had withdrawn from school, but the church group that I had been involved with on campus was planning a mission trip to Tijuana. They asked me to come along. I was spinning my wheels at home, the depression was lifting in fits and starts. I needed something to do. I had picked up some odd jobs like lawn mowing and landscaping. Hard labor was getting old real fast. I hate weeding. My parents were supportive of the idea. They wanted me out of the house, doing something, anything. Anything besides the depressed state that scared the hell out of all of us. My dad took me to California. He thought a change of scenery would help.

He had some work reason or other for being there. We went to Esalen. It is like boomer hippie heaven there. There were stream-fed tubs that people soaked in nude while watching the sun set over the Pacific coast. It was iconically featured in the last episode of *Mad Men*. Esalen's heyday was in the sixties, but boomers and their children still came here for workshops on spirituality, yoga, enlightenment, and psychology. This is all stuff that would typically interest me—that, and all the hot hippie chicks around. But instead I found myself preoccupied with whether I would die if I jumped off the cliff. I wasn't interested in being seriously maimed to live and tell the tale. I wanted to die. It seemed better not to risk it. I might not die, but there is a good chance I would be a paraplegic if I didn't. I decided I liked walking, while I was still alive anyway. That's the thing, even in this paradise with pretty nude women bathing with a view of the sun setting over the ocean, hanging out with my chill dad that I adored, and being freed from the responsibilities of school, I still wanted to die. Depression fucks you up. I spent a lot of time looking over that cliff at the rocks below.

Later on that trip an idea flashed through my mind. Maybe it was the Zoloft kicking in. Maybe it was the kindling of the hypomania that was to follow. I called my friend ███. He was in transition as well. He had withdrawn from college and had been going to flight school. He was as unmoored as I was. We had been best buddies in middle school, drifted apart in high school, but always were close whenever we saw each other. He was later in my wedding. I spoke at his dad's funeral. No matter how many years go by, we fall right back into joking around like 12-year-olds eating buttermilk pancakes at his mom's kitchen counter.

Suddenly I was far from the cliff, lifted up in the air. I remember standing next to a palm tree next to a motel pool surrounded by a tall white fence. Bathed in the California sun of my birth, everything seemed possible again. I had worked it all out. We'd join the church group to build a house in Tijuana and then we'd keep going south on our own. The church group was taking a Greyhound from our hometown to San Diego. The Mexican version of Greyhound would take us all the way to Cabo San Lucas. We could stop and stay at hostels on our way. It wasn't much of a plan, and I don't recall a budget being discussed. We reserved a few hostels and packed our bags.

The land that God forgot

Mexico was humbling. The place we worked had been dubbed "the land that God forgot." Miles and miles of shanty villages that had built up around the border when NAFTA loosened trade restrictions between the US and Mexico. These were the workers that worked in those factories. Homes made of tarp and garage doors were the upscale ones. Trash and stray dogs were everywhere. The people were lovely. We had a good time. I felt useful. I was actually making a tangible difference in the world of this family. I could see it in their grateful tears when we handed them the keys. ███ was handier than I am—he quickly was tapped for the more complex jobs like roofing and framing. I was good for hammering nails and befriending the soon-to-be owners of this 10x10 house, by far the nicest home for miles. The poverty of my childhood paled in comparison. We had our own beds, food to eat (occasionally from the food bank), medical care (even if paid for by the state), and decent schools near our home. These people appeared to have nothing, and yet they still smiled and laughed and were eking out a life here that had some meaning and purpose, despite the struggle. Me and my demons and my heartbreak in my dorm room had nothing on the real desolation here.

We stayed at a church that had rooms with bunk beds. We walked to the local market and they sold us beer. We were only 19! I still remember sipping the sweet smooth light bitterness from that green bottle of Modelo. Far from the wealthy coast of California, this place felt like heaven to me. This beer tasted like freedom. I wanted to live.

Losing it

A friend from my freshman dorm was on the trip. She had
dated a close friend of mine and was always super cool to me. I
was really glad she came along. I tried to set her up with ████.
They seemed to get along, but no one was sneaking off together
after the sun went down. Then one night I was sitting alone in
the living room area of our lodging. There was a big worn out
brown lazy boy in the middle of a big open room. I'm honestly
not even sure if there was glass in the windows. I was writing
in my journal, or pretending to. My friend, a lovely well-en-
dowed blonde with a sparkling smile, slipped into the room. I
heard her bare feet scratching across the concrete floor. She was
wearing a long summer dress, fresh from a well-deserved shower after our long work day in the dirt and the sun. She looked
beautiful in a way I had never noticed before. She sat on the arm
of the chair and gave me a light punch on the arm. We talked
about the day, about the people we had met and the poverty
and dignity that these people still carried. She slipped into my
lap. We were laughing and chatting but I noticed another feeling
creeping in. She noticed it too. My face flushed when I saw her
eyes grow when she felt the throbbing on her thigh. She didn't
move. She sat back and looked at me quizzically. "You're a virgin, aren't you?" My face turned even redder. "Ummm, yeah."

My braces in my senior year of high school and freshman year
of college hadn't helped in that department. But my teeth were
straight now, as it turned out I was. In high school I became
certain I must be gay. The attributes in the locker room that the
jocks described as being for faggots definitely applied to me. I
was shy and sensitive. I liked to read and would go to a stage
play over a football game anytime. I quit the soccer team to be
the lead in the school musical. I wasn't very athletic or good at
fixing things. I was weak and hated the part of gym class where
we had to lift weights. I pretty much hated all of gym class,
except badminton and bowling. Those were the sports for me. I
liked watching figure skating with my grandmother.

Girls certainly hadn't paid much attention to me, despite some emotionally devastating unrequited crushes that I never said a word to. But despite definitely fitting, in my mind, the gay description, there was one big problem. I found women very attractive.

My friends and I had first discovered sex in the early nineties when we got dial-up internet. For those digital natives that came along after this stone age of technology, the internet came through funny gurgly noises on the phone line. You couldn't use the phone at the same time you were online. And it was really slow. Streaming video was a faraway dream. But there were boobs. Lots of free pictures of boobs. Our parents were excited to bring all of this information to our fingertips, oh the learning, oh the academic heights the internet would take our developing minds to. That was all fine and good and something to keep open in a tab if a parent came in the room, but we went straight for the boobs. On a dial-up connection, one photo could take a few minutes to load. There, in those painfully long waits for boobs, and even longer for legs, I was seduced by internet porn. The first day I got to college, I plugged my laptop into the high speed T-1 line in my private dorm room. I was blown back by the sheer enormity and quick access I now had to all the boobs I could imagine. Porn with a high-speed internet connection is like mainlining heroin instead of eating a poppyseed muffin. Both can be quite pleasant, but one gets you there a lot faster. But as diverting as it was, I really wanted a partner to explore with - but all of the guys that seemed not at all gay were the ones getting the girls.

My orientation was making himself more and more known—so physically obvious it could no longer be ignored. Being a boy during puberty is like walking a narcoleptic pit bull on a leash. One minute he is sleeping and the next he is flexing his muscles, jaws dripping, ready to pounce and thrust and do what nature calls him to do. And then the object of desire disappears and he is asleep again. It is exhausting. I remember sitting behind a nice cheerleader in math class. She looked back and smiled at me. I could barely breathe. I was so grateful that I had a big textbook to carry over my lap as we walked out of class. She smiled and said "Bye ▇▇▇ see you tomorrow" and sashayed away, that pleated short blue and white skirt swaying as she bounced off. The pit bull went wild. She must have thought I really liked math. I was holding onto that book really tight. So it turns out I wasn't gay. I really liked girls, even more than I liked musical theatre. In hindsight, I was hanging out with a lot of girls in my extracurricular activities. I was the romantic lead and we had to practice those kisses a lot during rehearsal. Sure, there are a lot of gay guys into theatre—and thank god because I have a lot more in common with them than most straight guys — but theatre is full of smart dorky pretty girls. My type. And despite their friendships with the other guys on stage, I was the only one hiding behind textbooks in the dressing room. But despite some heavy petting, I still had a cherry that was ripe for popping.

That hot night in Mexico is burned into my memory. She had a twinkle in her eye. Her question about my virginity and my humiliating answer were ringing over and over in my ears. I felt like a deer in headlights. "Well, do you want to not be?" She gave me a come hither look. My jaw dropped. Holy shit!!! My pants were at full mast. I nodded, unable to get the words out. "Do you have a condom?" I nodded again. Did I have a condom???? Ummm, yeah…. I was hoping to explore other vices besides beer in Mexico. My cherry was ready to burst. I raised a finger to ask her for a moment.

I scampered out of the room, tucking my eager companion into the waistband of my shorts. Holy shit. This is it. I was rummaging through my bag…they must have been at the bottom. I wasn't expecting to need them on church grounds. My friend groaned and looked at me scoldingly when I turned on the light. He put a pillow over his head as my fingers felt the ribbed aluminum wrapper. I turned off the light and hurried back. My heart was beating fast but my friend, incredible hulking just moments before, had curled up into a soft ball. My breath seized. What if I couldn't do it… couldn't perform!? I had never had trouble by myself, but that was a lot less variables to control for.

But then I saw her smiling at me. Her fingers under her dress. She was ready for me. This wasn't her first time. She smiled invitingly.

I remember the condom was red. She helped me put it on and then sat me back in the chair and slid down. She wasn't wearing any panties. She was so soft and warm. Her breasts, her lips. I was so glad this first time was with her, someone I knew and trusted, someone I loved. Not some random hookup with a stranger. However random this hookup was, we had a connection. I don't think I lasted long. She was sympathetic and held my face in her soft breasts for what felt like an eternity. I was baffled as to what to do with the condom, but finally I settled on flushing it down the toilet. She kissed me goodnight and slipped off to bed. There I was, still alone with my journal, but forever altered. I was in a dazed blissful state. There's nothing like the real thing.

The next day I felt super awkward. Everyone complaining about the clogged toilet didn't help me forget why. Was she my girlfriend now, should I try to make her my girlfriend? Would I be an asshole if I didn't, would she feel used? So much for the short-lived bliss of last night. I had no idea what was going on in her mind. She was acting the same way she always had... super cool. And I'd always been comfortable around her... but now I was freaking out about what the hell to do. I was raised to be a gentleman and that sex was supposed to be a special thing with someone you loved and respected. She fit the bill, but I never really had girlfriend feelings about her, whatever those were. I think they usually involved getting caught up in fantasies about babies and mortgages and growing old together. I just liked hanging out with her. We only had one day left before she headed back north and ███ and I went south on our adventure. I decided that we were friends and that was all. She seemed good with that, but we never really talked about it.

Mexican Greyhound

The next thing I knew ███ and I were drinking a bucket of Coronas in Tijuana and waiting for our bus. The Mexican version of the Greyhound was decidedly different. The first stop was a hostel a few hundred miles south of Tijuana. It was called Coyote Cal's. The price was right, and the pictures on the website looked cool. It was just a short walk from the main highway, just a few miles. This seemed like a totally reasonable plan when I had dreamed it up in California.

It was pitch dark. ███ was snoring, drooling on my shoulder. The bus shuddered to a stop. The driver got up and pointed at us, motioning to the door. I held out the address to be sure. He nodded profusely. All I could see was darkness. When we stepped off the bus I saw a dirt road snaking into the dark. The driver pointed at the road. He opened up the side of the bus and then demanded money. We were definitely not stateside anymore. ███ was ready to put up a fight, still grumpy that he was awoken from his peaceful slumber. But I paid and he gave us our bags.

I wanted to get on with our adventure and I wasn't going to let any third-world corruption get in our way. We started down the empty dirt road. The bus drove off. We were bathed in darkness. The stars were bright and luminous. "Ummm... how far is it?" ███ asked. Too dark to see the guidebook now, I say "A mile or two...they said it wasn't far." We kept walking and it got darker and darker the farther we got from the highway. We were tired. The Corona had long worn off and we were still sore from the hard labor in Tijuana from the days before.

From the outside we were a couple of sleepy young men with backpacks, wandering down a dirt road toward what we had been told would soon be the ocean. From the inside it felt crazy and scary and wild and amazing. The light chill of the spring night kissing my skin...I felt alive and certain of nothing but this moment. The plan had been destroyed. College, goals, hopes, dreams, depression. Those weren't here. There was only me, my friend, and the Mexican darkness.

We started to get cold, hungry and tired of walking. A few cars had passed, but none had stopped. I started to consider sleeping in a field. And then we saw another set of headlights. They were coming from behind us but approaching fast. We moved to the side of the road. A truck came flying off the main highway. We waved them down, and twenty feet past us they dug a hole in the gravel when the driver slammed on the breaks. We showed them the address to our hostel and they nodded, as if they knew all about it. They motioned to the back and we happily obliged.

Suddenly we were bouncing along in the back of a pickup truck in the Mexican night. As the headlights licked the sharp twists and turns of the potholed road, I started to notice crosses and flowers set up all along the side of the road. They were the type that memorialize someone who died in an accident there. Bottles were flying out of the driver's window. I gulped as I watched the driver crack another beer and tip his cowboy hat in our direction. My companion and I looked at each other with wide eyes that spoke of terror and sheer exhilaration. We dug into our backpacks and found a couple of beers and cracked them open…we were on the roller coaster…so we might as well join in the fun. We clinked bottles and yelled MEXICO!

That trip was almost 20 years ago now, and I am grateful to have memories and photos and journal entries to document the trip. The hostel didn't disappoint. We went deep sea fishing and I caught a giant white fish that we drowned in beer. We bought tortillas and limes and ate fish tacos for days. We continued on the bus to Mulege, then La Paz, then Cabo San Lucas. We went to the beach and the clubs. Our pasty white bodies burned and then tanned. We danced and drank and met an interesting cast of ex-pats. "Margaritaville" was on heavy rotation wherever we went. I smiled at a lot of girls and they smiled back. If I had known during my high school foreign language class the sheer amount of beautiful Latina female companionship I would have had if my Spanish was passable… I would have studied harder.

I went to the movies in La Paz with a Mexican girl I had met at a club and we made out the whole time. She had braces. The film was "The Mexican" with Brad Pitt and Julia Roberts. It was in English with Spanish subtitles. I laughed out loud several times to a silent theatre, before the rest of the room erupted in chuckles. There was a slight delay in the subtitles. She was nice but the conversation was a bit hard to keep up, with her limited English and my even more limited Spanish.

████ and I took a boat to a popular beach near Cabo San Lucas. We had all of our bags and he volunteered to watch our stuff while I looked around for a good place for us to sit and chill. ████ came wandering up and I became irate that he had left our bags alone. There was a reason that the military patrolled these beaches with assault rifles. They're not safe. "It's ok man, I left them with this guy and his kid, he said he'd keep an eye on them." I was not convinced, my bare feet pressing into the warm sand as I jogged back to where we had come in on the boat. I immediately felt better when I spotted our bags. He was right. This guy with gray hair looked like a college professor. I think he *was* a college professor. He and his 8-year-old kid were playing Magic cards. They were totally safe with this guy. The funny thing, I just realized, is my friend and I are those guys now. We could just as likely be sitting on a beach somewhere playing cards with one of our kids, clearly the most responsible ones around, and some vagabonds might trust us with their only belongings.

The tacos caught up with my friend. He got food poisoning. He spent the night on the toilet. I spent the night in a club. I felt great. The next day we snorkeled off a private beach. The credit card my dad had given me for emergencies only had a hold put on it for the gear, that they promised would be taken off when we returned it. My dad's credit card company called him about the strange foreign charge totaling a couple thousand dollars. He cancelled the card assuming I must have had the card lost or stolen. Safety net gone, we were burning through pesos. We ran out of money. We called our parents. We needed to get to San Diego to get to the closest Western Union to be wired some more cash. We had bus tickets but no food. We panhandled, asking tourists for money. I had never done that and haven't since. It was humiliating and thrilling all at once. We bought peanut butter and tortillas and got on the bus. We went north, over the border, and back to our safe, predictable hometown in the Pacific Northwest.

World Traveler

We got home and I was no longer a college dropout. When people asked me what I was up to, I no longer had to hide my head in shame and talk about my failure at college and my inability to embrace landscaping as my chosen profession. I was a world traveler! This was my identity now. I was writing and had big plans to share my adventures in a book or series of articles someday soon.

I spent the summer as a camp counselor in the Appalachian Mountains, where I had worked the previous summer and attended as a kid. I enjoyed the company of hippie girls. I plotted a new exotic adventure. In the fall I planned to work construction with a buddy until my plane left for Thailand on September 12, 2001. As it turned out, no planes were taking off that day. I distinctly remember seeing the headline that someone had flown into the World Trade Center and reflexively thought, "What idiot would fly their Cessna into a building in downtown New York?" Little did I know that this act would lead to an endless world war on terror, and profoundly impact a dear friend of mine who went to the front lines in Iraq. But I didn't know any of that then.

I was just really annoyed because they grounded all the planes. I was a traveler! My international trip was rescheduled a week. Good thing I didn't have any other plans. I made a few hundred more bucks doing construction. My college buddy had signed up to do a work study school project in Bali and planned to stop in Thailand along the way. He invited me to go. I needed a passport for this trip. My first passport! I was definitely in.

Planes started taking off again, and after a layover in Seoul, we touched down in Bangkok. Soon we were on a ferry destined for a tropical island. We saw my dear cousin ██, back when things were simpler and her mom and sister were still alive. A few years later we would all be in Thailand together for her destination wedding.

But this time we were all young and single and free. My cousin was teaching English to a group of police officers. They loved my red hair. The chief took us out for karaoke. We danced at half moon parties and snorkeled in warm blue turquoise water and ate pad Thai every day. We rode scooters along palm-lined coastal roads. It was truly paradise.

Years later I wrote a feature-length screenplay titled *Paradise* based on my experiences there. The closest it has been to the screen is collecting dust on top of my DVD player. I would happily option it to anyone who offers me and my family an all expenses paid trip to Thailand to watch the filming. But this book isn't about Thailand. I was entirely too sane there to discuss it in this book. I had worried that I might go off the deep end in the sex capital of the world, but I kept it in my pants. Some strange encounters, but no regrets. A young man on an adventure for sure, but I stayed out of trouble.

Extended Family

Freshly tanned from Thailand, I headed to the opposite climate. I went to the Midwest. My uncle put me to work ripping up carpet and painting the interior of his house. A dear old family friend, ██ ██, also needed my help to sort through the massive collection of her late husband's books and papers. It was fucking freezing. But there was great company. The bonds cemented during that time served me later in life. ██ died recently at 98. She is most definitely singing with the angels and teaching piano lessons in heaven.

In the spring I went back east to stay with my sisters. I got to know them better. My brother-in-law got me a job at a pizza place. My sister's friend and former professor, a licensed clinical social worker, broke her leg and I became her chauffeur. "Driving Miss ███," my sister often joked. Her job as a therapist sounded pretty cool. I started to realize what the career prospects were for a college dropout, and international travel was expensive. I applied to go back to college in the fall. Life was back on track.

7

Blonde

Some old friends from college wanted to rent a house together. They heard I was coming back and invited me to live with them. We looked at a lot of funky rentals that appealed to college students like us. We finally settled on a black house with purple trim. It was rumored to be owned by a goth dentist, who people had sworn to have seen snorting cocaine in the local bars or off the dashboard of his white Camaro. The price was right. It was a two-bedroom with a big living room. ███ and ████ were together, so they got one room. ███ and I were single so we would rotate in and out of the living room. We put up shower curtains to create a separate space. The living room person paid less rent. I was the first up in the living room. It was like a really big fort. I loved it.

It was good to be living with friends who were hilarious and smart and cared about me. But I remember many walks to the bus on gray wet mornings that were very hard. The depression that I had worked so hard to overcome was not far away. I could feel it, chilling me to the bone. My biggest fear was that it would happen again, catch me when I least expected it. But I was enjoying my studies, more sociology and history and religion than political economy. I was working on a project at the local cable access TV station and meeting more people. There was a spring trip to South America that we were all eagerly anticipating. More freedom at the end of another dark winter. I went home for the holidays, nervous about coming back to the dark rainy lonely days in my college town. But then I was reminded that I had friends. I was invited to parties. I could go to bars. I kept going to class. I got good marks on my papers. I made a documentary.

I might just make it through another full year of college. It was also the first time I had been in college with no braces. I had dated a little bit but nothing serious, nothing more than kissing. Girls seemed to be noticing me but I was too awkward to ever pursue many of them. I wanted a girlfriend, a lover, a companion. The girls I was seeing didn't seem to want this, with me anyway.

And then my friend invited me to a party at the campus theatre where he worked. He was tending bar and promised to overserve me. It was a costume party and he had keys to the costume shop. I was single and ready to mingle. My memories of that night are hazy. My friend kept his promise about the overserving, and I certainly mingled. I chatted and danced with some ladies, but didn't feel much chemistry and moved along through the crowd. And then I saw an elegant swan dressed in a velvet purple dress dancing with a female friend of mine from my freshman dorm. It was loud, so I'm not sure if we could even hear each other yell, but my friend pulled me in to dance with them. Before long the blonde in velvet and I were dancing close.

There was certainly a spark, despite her spurning my advances. At some point in the evening I crinkled a piece of paper into her hand with my phone number on it and whispered, "If you don't want to make love…then maybe we can have lunch sometime." The next thing I remember is my friends dragging me out of there before I made too much more of a fool of myself. It should be noted that she reports an entirely different version of the events of the evening.

I woke up the next morning laughing, some vague memory that I had had fun and made a bit of a fool out of myself. Good thing that girl had graduated and just moved to ██████, a two hour drive away. She was in town for one last hurrah. She also happened to be getting out of a relationship with a guy that I knew — but I didn't know they went together at the time. When I mentioned her name to my roommate's brother over coffee in our kitchen he said, "Oh, you mean ███'s girlfriend?" ███ was huge. Like WWE huge. He had always been friendly to me, but I knew he would crush me like a fried cricket if he found out that I was hitting on his girlfriend. Just as all color drained from my face, ██████ walked in and informed us that they had officially broken up a week ago. I exhaled audibly. They laughed heartily as the terrified look on my face receded.

Relieved, I was ready to start the day—go out for breakfast and studying. Move on. We headed downtown to ████'s Bagels, which is sadly no longer there. We sat at a table and I was reading my sociology textbook, highlighter at the ready. My friend went outside to smoke a cigarette. I glanced up from my book and my heart sank. There, talking with my friend were the girls that I had been dancing with at the party last night. ████ and I had been friends since freshman year; not super close, but she knew I was a good guy.

The blonde was supposed to have left town. All of the humor that I had awoken to about the prior night was gone. I looked for a back exit. There was none. She was coming in. They walked in and got in line. I stared at my book, but she spotted me. And she spotted me spotting her. With no other option but to throw myself on the mercy of the court, I walked up to her and said "hi." I'm sure my face was as red as my hair at that point. She smiled a wide sparkling grin and said "hi." I was confused. My whole life I had been trained to be a nice guy and not shamelessly hit on women, and then the night I drink enough to lose those inhibitions, I hit on one that doesn't seem to mind? I stand there speechless for what felt like forever, inhibitions and nice-guyness fully re-established. "Don't be creepy, don't be creepy, don't be creepy" ran through my mind, a common mantra since I had become aware of the fraught relationship between the sexes and been trained not to be "one of those guys." Thankfully she had her wits about her, otherwise the guy at the deli counter would have soon been mopping me off the floor. "Why don't we start over," she smiled and blushed and put out her hand. "I'm █████." This girl was charming and even prettier in the daytime.

Surprised, I stepped back but offered her a firm businesslike handshake with no creepy lingering at all. I said something stupidly obvious like "I'm ████ and…umm…we're sitting over there," gesturing to the table with my textbook. I wasn't sure if I should invite her over or if that would be creepy too. "Don't be creepy, play it cool, play it cool." My brain was coaching me. This is the brain that had never even had a serious girlfriend, or dated a girl seriously for more than a couple of months for that matter. Maybe I shouldn't listen to him. "Can we join you?" she said, blushing slightly. "Ummm, yeah, yeah sure, we have more chairs." I walked back to the table and almost tripped while pulling another chair from an empty table. I sat and pretended to look at my book for an eternity while they finished waiting in line and ordering. ████ sat across from me. I have no idea what we talked about. What I remember is that I played it very cool and was very not creepy at all. I am well-trained to be the nicest boy in school that everyone's mom hopes you hang out with. I tried really hard not to be the drunken Don Juan from the previous night, but I was confused. Maybe she was just nice…but she was really nice. She seemed into me…like really into me. I was really confused. She was leaving town in a few hours. This girl had potential, she was gorgeous, blonde, tall, smart, funny, and I had already made a fool out of myself with her and she was still talking to me. I had to get her to stay another day.

My friend and his new girlfriend were traveling to Europe for the following quarter and we were throwing him a goodbye party at the bar down the street. I not-so-subtly hinted and then not-at-all-creepily begged, then pleaded her to come out for a drink. She did know my friend after all. How did all of my friends know this girl and I had never met her?

I sipped a microbrew at the bar, determined not to repeat the buffoonery of the previous evening. It was a funky place with velvet-covered booths and a wood-paneled bar full of every type of booze you could imagine. I glanced furtively at the door, hoping that she would walk through it. Finally I gave up and went to the bathroom. When I returned she was sitting at a table with my friends laughing and drinking a beer. I took the seat across from her. We joked around and played Connect Four. I played it really cool. There was a lot of eye contact.

She had to go. I knew it was now or never. I walked her to her car. And then for some reason I got into the passenger seat. Maybe it was cold outside. I pinned myself against the window, not wanting to make her uncomfortable being too close to this strange young man that she had just let into her car. It got quiet and you could cut the tension with a knife. Our cheeks flushed in unison. We both audibly laughed an awkward laugh. And then she looked me in the eyes with a twinkle in hers and said "If you wanted to kiss me, now would be a good time." My eyes popped and I held my breath. I involuntarily nodded and moved my hand to her face. Her breath was hot and her lips were wet. We made out like teenagers in heat. She gave me her phone number and dropped me back off at the bar. She had a long drive ahead of her. She promised to come back soon. I stepped onto the sidewalk and waved as she drove off. Her windows were entirely fogged up, from the inside. I watched the glowing red rear lights of that white Volvo wagon until it turned, and she was gone.

What followed was a brief but intense six-week affair. I took a Greyhound to visit her, she drove to my house a handful of times. We bonded over our lactose intolerance, our love of theatre, and our families' background in politics. She listened to my big dreams and was attracted to my ambition. I broke her bed. We went through a few boxes of condoms. One time we were having a party at the black house and the police came to the door asking to speak to the person whose house it was. Someone knocked on my bedroom door. I had rotated out of the living room fort just in time to need a private place to entertain a high-class lady. ████ and I came out flushed and wearing different clothes than we had walked in with, she in my t-shirt. I promised the cops that we would keep it down, I turned on the responsible white boy charm. He gave me a wink when the pretty blonde came and took my hand and pulled me back into the bedroom. I got a cheer from the crowd. She was classy and sexy and smart and hot for me. I felt good about myself when I was with her. We had a lot to talk about. She was sweet and her skin was oh so soft.

████ spoke German and French and she was a talented the-atre director. She came from a good home and was close to her still-married parents. She had a self-assuredness and grace that was reassuring and intimidating all at once. I was in middle school when she graduated from high school. I came from a broken home and was still sorting out who I was.

She was four years older than me and had just gotten out of a long-term relationship. I was a kid who'd just recovered from a bad bout of depression and had his braces off and wanted to have fun. It quickly dawned on me that this girl wanted to get married and have babies soon. This was minivan territory. She was the type of girl I could do that with, but I wasn't ready. She invited me to her brother's wedding. Her whole family would be there. She invited me to dinner at her parents' house. Sud-denly I was feeling a little over my head. I graciously declined the invitations.

I also had a study abroad trip planned to South America that was part of the course I had started in the fall. I had had romantic visions of sowing my wild oats with Latin women, of being free to do whatever and whoever I wanted. I was definitely taking the trip, I had paid for it and was looking forward to an adventure with the friends I had made in my class. My Chilean professor also had a bit of a wild reputation and I was looking forward to seeing him on his home turf.

I wanted lady freedom and she wanted me. I also wanted ████, but I wasn't ready for what she was offering. She was willing to keep it open-ended, not act like we were too serious. No commitment. We would do that in the hope of keeping in touch and rekindling things when I returned. I didn't feel right about that. I didn't want to leave her hanging and expecting more than I could give, I didn't want to leave my heart open to fall any deeper in love than I already had. I broke it off—clear as I could be that it was over. I felt like a jerk but it seemed like the right thing at the time. I have no regrets, well maybe a little bit…because I hurt someone that I loved, and still love. But I was free.

8

South America

Chile did not disappoint. We drank wine, toured spirit distill-
eries and cultural and industrial sites, and ate amazing food.
My pothead friends miraculously found marijuana immediately. They approached the first guy they saw on the street that
had dreadlocks and as quick as you could load a pipe, they
were high. Marijuana wasn't my thing, but the whole exchange
fascinated me. The international economics of the drug trade
fascinates me. Latin American countries are destroying themselves to supply drugs to the U.S., but here we came right to
the source. The seasons are opposite on the bottom side of the
world. Rainy spring in the Pacific Northwest was a warm fall in
Santiago. I loved walking the old streets and trying to speak in
my broken Spanish.

The locals were very nice, and curious about this tall redheaded young man from the north. Anyone that spoke English was eager to talk to me and my friends. In Santiago I stayed in the home of a lovely grandmother and her daughter and grandson. I had my own room. When I came home from the adventures of the day, the little boy, not more than 3 or 4, would run up to me and I would lift him in my arms. I felt the pull to have this experience with my own child someday. We made empanadas in her kitchen and laughed and smiled. We could barely communicate, but the languages of love and food and kindness are universal.

I became close with one of my classmates. She and I were not in the pot-smoking crowd. We bought suits and talked politics and the big political careers we dreamed of. We were working on a documentary about the U.S.'s influence on the Chilean economy. There was a complex, often dysfunctional, relationship between the Chilean and U.S. governments. After the Chilean people elected a socialist leader, the U.S. installed and supported a dictator named Pinochet whose fascist policies helped capitalism thrive and the wealth be distributed unevenly. My classmate had a boyfriend that seemed like more of an idea than a solid relationship and I was still pining for the girl back home.

We started hooking up. The other students would notice us slip off together for hours at a time, but we imagined we were being discreet. It was fun. She knew what she was doing in that department. But she had some problems. She started drinking too much and coming apart about the boy when he called and broke up with her. I remember holding her hair back as she threw up, feeling like I liked her, I cared for her, but we were more of friends with benefits than lovers. She had a lot going on with her family back home and this boy that broke up with her. I wasn't up for the drama right then. Suddenly hanging out with her was less exciting, it felt like my newfound freedom was being weighed down by baggage that wasn't my own. My friends advised me that she had some serious issues that I shouldn't take on myself. I pulled away physically but we continued our school project and remained friendly.

In the mornings I got up early and ran around the track next to the compound where we were staying. My thoughts swirled. I was running hot, or that is what I call it now. My thoughts get going and I have trouble sleeping. My heart races and I am more interested in big ideas and sex and changing the world. There is a grandiosity to it, this feeling that everything is possible. That I am amazing and nothing can stand in my way. My psychiatrist calls that feeling hypomania. It feels alive to me. Not stable, but not depressed. My anxiety spiked and my thoughts raced. I needed to bury myself in the arms of another woman, I needed to slow down. I was in the right place.

I was in Latin America surrounded by beautiful women who were noticing me. Not too many redheads around those parts, especially as tall and handsome and cocky as me at that moment. I started to frequent these espresso shops downtown. Roughly translated, they are called café con piernas or "coffee with legs"—a place for men, usually middle-aged, to talk to immodestly dressed flirtatious women. It was great. You just drank coffee and flirted and tipped big. Pretty innocent really. Much classier than the drive through bikini coffee stands that have popularized the outskirts of so many towns in the States. Drinking this hot coffee while conversing with a beautiful woman in a language whose basics I barely had a handle on, was thrilling for a boy from a small town like me. All that espresso probably didn't hurt my lift into hypomania either.

There was a gorgeous Argentinian woman that I enjoyed visiting. Her legs went on for miles and I could feel myself drowning in her eyes. She had done some modeling. I asked her out. We went to dinner. The steak was really good. The conversation was awkward. It soon became clear that the language barrier was too much to overcome. The heat, for me anyway, started to fade. It turns out that looks aren't everything, though I was kicking myself because this woman was smoking hot. As we pulled up in front of her place I debated in the taxi whether to ask to come in, but in the end we hugged and talked about me visiting Argentina. She said I would like her mom and her sister. That's me, the boy you want to bring home to meet the family.

I started going to another coffee shop. I ran into one of the men that worked at the compound where we had stayed when we first arrived in Chile. I remembered that he had a pretty daughter a few years older than me whose English was better than mine. He was funny and enjoyed practicing his English with me. He told me that this coffee shop sometimes had a special where all the men put in extra cash and they would close the blinds and the waitresses would dance around on the bar with their tops off. I had heard rumors of such places. I had cash in my pocket. I was in. It turned out to be my lucky day.

They locked the door and cranked up the music. The tits came out. My young blood boiled with passion and excitement. It was awesome. As we rode the bus home, the man and I replayed the events and laughed and giggled like middle school boys. He invited me for dinner and I happily joined. I loved Chilean food, wine, and company. It felt like being with family, family whose drama was in another language I didn't understand. I enjoyed talking to his daughter at dinner. She invited me to go to the zoo with her the next day. The elephants and lions and monkeys were exotic, but not nearly as exotic as my Latin companion.

She had hopes and dreams, loved literature and poetry, and her dark eyes and auburn hair sparkled in the sun. She introduced me to Neruda, the renowned Chilean poet. His words penetrated my soul. He wrote of the pain of being a man in the world. It was a pain that I thought that I had been fully immersed in. Little did I know how deep that well of human sorrow goes.

The speed of my thoughts were picking up. I talked faster, my anxiety spiked, I boiled over with passion for this country and its beautiful people. We kissed. We made out while the lions looked on. It bordered on heavy petting. I knew she wanted more. I did too. We caught a cab into town and she told me about a hotel that rented rooms by the hour, where executives take their secretaries for "off-site meetings" — a place where we could be alone.

"Sí, Sí," she called out. She apologized for slipping into Spanish, forgetting English in the heat of our passion. "No no, I like it!" I insisted. It was really really fucking hot. I had a Latin lover. The next few weeks were hot and heavy with her. She was hot for me and I was running hot in general. She was beautiful, smart, ambitious and kind but I didn't find any feelings catching beyond the sparks in the bedroom. I wasn't thinking about wedding bells or minivans or babies with her. I really enjoyed her company.

Between seeing her and frequenting yet another espresso bar, I continued my coursework and project. The girl from my class seemed jealous and the Chilean's girl's father's mood toward me cooled. Maybe no longer the boy to bring home? I have a bad feeling that karma will be a bitch when my daughters start dating.

As my time in Chile came to a close, I got an email from a girl that I knew from school. We had dated briefly the previous year and she was doing a project in Nicaragua. She knew I was in Chile and we had joked about me visiting her in Nicaragua, but at that point her plans weren't set. But she was there now. She invited me to come visit on my way home. It was totally on the way! And I had time. I talked my professor into another 8 credits for a paper I would write on the liberation theology and political economy of Nicaragua. He was in, especially when I mentioned the reason I was really going. My grandpa volunteered to buy me a plane ticket as soon as he heard a girl was involved. A widower and aspiring Don Juan himself, he was happy to live vicariously through his handsome grandson. By the time he was my age he had been married and settled down, not many opportunities to play the field when he was operating radios on a navy ship in the Pacific during WWII. I think my professor was in the same boat. I hope I am in a position someday to sponsor the foolish escapades of a young person pursuing love.

The school program in Chile came to a close. My classmates and I packed our bags and headed to the airport. I hugged the Chilean girl goodbye and promised to write, already knowing that I was headed into the arms of another woman. My classmates headed for their gate. We stopped and hugged and promised to meet back up at school. My ticket had been rerouted, my adventure was far from over. I boarded the plane for Nicaragua, my heart beating with the excitement and terror of heading out on my own into a third world country with only my passport, a backpack, and some traveler's checks. I was a world traveler, after all; this is what I do.

The girl was staying at a farm run by Maryknoller nuns in rural Nicaragua. I had always liked Catholics, though I had been raised loosely Protestant with a new-age twist. I've always liked older women too. My grandma and her friends loved to have me around and gush about how pretty my hair was. My mom talked about Jesus and reincarnation and god's universal love at home. I went to fundamentalist church conferences and Lutheran summer camp with friends, and went to the Methodist church on occasional Sundays with my mom and grandma. I was baptized and confirmed in the Methodist church when I was 12. I was down with people that followed Jesus, even if I wasn't quite sure what I believed anymore. Chile was so Catholic, and the Easter pageantry I had witnessed was enchanting. My grandparents were also Catholic, with an emphasis on family and social justice. I had been fascinated by the ritual of my dad's father's funeral a few months before. It is comforting to have a structured way to celebrate life and accept death. Grief is a very chaotic experience and I understand the need to create structure and ritual around it. The Catholics definitely got some things right. So when she invited me to come hang out with nuns and her in Nicaragua I was all in.

I got my eight credits, had a lovely time with the nuns, farmed the land, and was humbled by the quiet dignity of these very poor people. This girl was super smart, PhD in her future. Science smart, not the kind of smart that I am. I was enamored, crushing on her beauty and brilliance. She wouldn't let me get too close. She made it clear that we were just friends with benefits, nothing more. I knew I wanted more.

Stateside

I went back to my college town and moved out of the black house and into my aunt and uncle's basement. I took long walks, imagining that I might be governor some day. I made grand speeches under my breath. The only way I could make a real difference was to do something big and bold and ambitious like that. I obsessed about it. I did a lot of cardio at the gym. My mind was constantly grinding away on my ambitious plans. I had to make something of myself. I was still running hot. All summer I walked to the nearby YMCA where I was a counselor for a middle school day camp.

It was a fun way to spend my days, but my nights were lonely after such a passionate spring, the heat of those women was still boiling in my body. The girl returned from Nicaragua. I had become a vegetarian and had started exercising more, hoping to impress her. I had moved into my own studio apartment. It quickly became clear that she had no interest in being my girlfriend. It became clear that friendship wasn't really on the table either. I sensed that maybe she had had a Latin lover after I left. I was crushed and withdrew, afraid to run into her on campus because of the intense turmoil she triggered within me. In hindsight, it really wasn't about her. But she became the object of my obsession that soon turned into another crippling depression.

I enrolled in an intensive 16-credit political economy program. It was a similar one to the one I had been taking when I dropped out two years before. One of the professors was the same. I was determined to face the challenge again, and after my recent experiences in countries with developing economies, I had more context for my studies. It truly interested me. But the Marxist slant of my professors was overwhelming for someone that wanted to make a difference in the world. Nothing but absolute revolt would make our economy socialist, make our world fair and just. My mind spun and spun. So many problems in the world to fix, how do I help? The reading was plentiful and dense. I couldn't keep up. I was so overwhelmed, crushed by my own sense of responsibility and my growing awareness of the complex problems our world was facing.

Midway through fall quarter I knew it was happening again. Those dreaded feelings of depression were creeping in. It was more and more of a struggle to get out of bed and on the bus to class. I spent most of my time alone, in my head. When with friends I would sit in the corner and ruminate. My friend, back from Europe, asked me if I was ok. He knew of my past struggles with depression. He walked with me to the campus health center. I told the doctor how I was feeling and she offered to write a prescription for Zoloft at the previous dose I had been on. I had tapered off of it on my own before I went to Chile. I begrudgingly filled the prescription.

I had requested an appointment with the school counseling center weeks before and they finally called to offer me an appointment. The Tibetan Buddhist counselor encouraged meditation and gave me a book called *Feeling Good*, about cognitive behavioral therapy. It sat on my nightstand while I stared at the ceiling thinking about all of my failures, all of my future failures, that I couldn't do it, that I would never have a career or a family or an adult life. I wished that I would fall asleep and never wake up. I wish that I had had the energy or motivation to read that book. I have since read it and recommended it to clients. It is really practical and helpful. But at that moment nothing offered solace. There was no hope for me. The passionate heights I had climbed to down south were like a dream now, far out of reach. The bright colors of fall in Latin America were replaced by the grayscale of another Northwest winter.

9

Hello Again

Reunion

I saw her. I was walking by the shops downtown and saw her
in the window behind the counter of one. There was a closed
sign in the window but I tried to open the door. It was locked
but I knocked. She saw me, her eyes narrowing like a blow
dart gun. She shrugged her shoulders and lifted her hands,
acting like she didn't have the keys. I walked off, shaking my
head, puzzled. I had sworn that I had seen her car drive by me,
the woman driving by scowling at me. But that woman was a
redhead, not the blonde whose arms I had fallen asleep in six
months before. But there she was, in that shop, it was definitely her. She was a redhead now. I gave up and walked off.
I guess that was over; she clearly never wanted to talk to me

again, and I didn't blame her.

I ran into her on the street a few days later. I played it cool but
was surprised that she was a little warmer. She invited me to
breakfast. Then she invited me to a play. It was funny and I
laughed harder than I had in weeks. I tried to play it cool, not
trying to make any moves, but she took my hand and asked
for a tour of my apartment. My little apartment had never been
warmer than it was that night. I made smoothies in the morning. She seemed surprised, still suspecting that I was just using
her for a booty call. I make really good smoothies. I still make
her one almost every day.

Testing

████ and I were spending most nights together. She was con-
sidering birth control and our condom budget was running low.
We both did the responsible thing and got STD tested. I was
eager to try unprotected sex.

It was an awkward trip to the public health department. I went
alone. A diverse mix of folks in the lobby. Other people without
health insurance like me. The front desk had given me a clip-
board and paperwork to complete, including how many sexual
partners I had had in my lifetime. I remember being unshaven
in a knit hat, recovering from a cold and pretty depressed. I
was feeling far from sexy, far from the charming guy that had
fucked his way through Latin America. The number neared the
double digits, which didn't include the ones I had merely kissed
or engaged in heavy petting with. I had not long ago been a
virgin, embarrassed when people brought up sex and assumed I
was in the club. Definitely not a virgin now!

The nurse was a woman in her 50s with short hair. I curiously
wondered if was a lesbian. She peered down at the papers I had
filled out. She squinted her eyes, put on reading glasses to check
again what I had written. She looked skeptically at me. "You've
been busy," was all she said. She took my blood and confirmed
that I had no symptoms of any STIs and went on her way. I re-

member feeling a bit embarrassed. Just months before my blood had boiled with heat and passion and desire. Now they were testing it for deadly diseases. Had I just been young and horny or was it a sign of something more, the hypomania before my crash into depression?

I continue to question it—the clearest period of potential hypomania in my history. My psychiatrist had started asking more questions about my "up" periods, the times when I "ran hot," as I sometimes described it. Do typical people have that much sex with that many people in a year, or is it just those that have a diagnosable condition? I certainly imagined there were others, especially men, who had had a period of being as slutty as me, but is it a sign of illness or just virility? A stallion collecting stories? I'm far from a stallion, just a sensitive kid dropping panties with poetry and wild sad eyes. I figured I'd settle down at some point, but I had wanted to wet my whistle first.

██ was the only woman I wanted to be with now. I left the others behind. I think I am probably an asshole in someone else's story. The guy that never called, never wrote, after the heated affair(s). But I wasn't just in it for the sex; I craved the connection, the intimacy, the intelligence of the beautiful women that let me get so close, let me inside. But some I had wanted more than wanted me, and others had wanted more than I could give. None of them were quite right. This Goldilocks had finally come back to the bed that fit. When we bought our wedding rings, the jeweler said "There's a lot of love in this house," as he gestured around the glittering store to all the couples shopping for high-priced symbols of their commitment. ██ and I often still say that line to each other. As crazy as she makes me sometimes, she is the one whose arms I want to be in at the end of the day.

10

Halfway House

Before I ever officially went to the day hospital, I stayed in a halfway house of sorts, many years before. One of the teams in the organization I work for is focused on a "hospital at home" model of care, where physically fragile people can be closely monitored and supported to heal in the comfort of their own home. Before I even knew there was such a thing as a psychiatric day hospital, I had been in a hospital at home.

When we reunited, ████'s dad was dying of cancer. She had moved home to take care of him. She was renting a studio apartment just a few blocks up the hill from mine. Despite having her to be with me in my loneliness, I continued my descent into depression. It was scary. I was losing interest and ability to contribute in class. I stopped going. The medication wasn't helping. I felt worse. I called in sick a lot to my job at the school president's office—a competitive job that I had worked hard to get. I didn't care. I just walked in the rain or lay in my bed and ruminated, obsessing about the past and the future, my soul as gloomy as the winter skies. When walking by the marina I wondered what it would take to drown myself.

The song "Crazy" by Gnarls Barkley rings true whenever I hear it on the radio, because when you lose your shit, you are no longer bound to the convention and expectations of being normal and stable. It is a relief to let go of all that pressure. In my experience, in order to recover and heal, you actually have to accept the crazy, accept that you are no longer high-functioning, that maybe you are barely functioning, if you are functioning at all.

I'm not sure what happened exactly. The floor had once again dropped out from under me, and I was hanging by a thread. I was at the library googling "how to tie a noose" and eyeing the fire escape attached to the back of my apartment building. One day I broke down and admitted to ███ how suicidal I was feeling. She asked me. I didn't volunteer it. She could see how much I was struggling. I had told her about what happened several years before in the bathtub. She asked me directly if I had a plan to hurt myself. I nodded. She called my dad and drove me to his house an hour away.

Before long I was officially having a nervous breakdown. I tried to pull it back together, I took more Zoloft, but I just felt worse and worse. I was crashing and burning. It was happening again. I couldn't go back to school. Dad offered me a room in his house. I withdrew from school. Dad, freshly divorced, was renting a place with my brother, freshly out of jail. And so I moved into this halfway house of sorts. It was a place for recovery, I hoped. We all did.

While my brother was working the deli counter at the local health food store it was all I could do to drag myself on to the bus to my twice-weekly appointments with my new psychologist. I couldn't sleep at night, would lie there with my mind racing, and then lay in bed much of the day trying to catch the sleep that had run away from me the night before. What little shred of pride I had was fading fast. I sucked it up and accepted a referral to a psychiatrist.

11

Hello Lithium,
My Old Friend

The Monday after I finished at the day hospital I went back to work. I slipped quietly into my cubicle and opened my email. Most people in the office just thought I had been on vacation, if they knew I was gone at all. Our remote work policy is pretty loose. Quite often the office is a ghost town, as people frequently work from home. My boss doesn't even work in my office; most of my meetings with him are on the phone. I spoke with the few people that I had told the real reason for my time off and assured them I was feeling better. Honestly, I wasn't feeling way better, but I felt like I had to act like I was.

The funny thing was I'm not sure if they even knew there was really anything wrong in the first place, so maybe the difference was subtle anyway. Or maybe they had been watching me fade away for months, but didn't know how to ask if I was ok since they could tell I was so committed to pretending I was fine. Maybe they were relieved I got help and glad I was feeling better.

Before long I settled back into the rhythm of work and it felt manageable. I decided not to resume my side work until the new year. I wasn't doing anything extra, and was seeing that the significant effort I had put in earlier in the year was paying off and maybe I could slide for a while, through the holidays anyway. I started cooking dinner again. I played with my children. I took walks. I was still tired and watching a lot of TV and eating a lot of chocolate, but I wasn't depressed. I wanted to live. The dark thoughts left.

I'm not sure if the new cocktail of meds finally synergized, if the time off and lifestyle changes I am making are bearing fruit, or if just the passage of time heals all wounds. My psychiatrist said as much at our last appointment. We are both relieved, no matter the reason, that I am out of the woods. Weekly appointments turn into monthly as stability takes hold and I come back for refills and to share my progress and the still human, however stable, challenges of my day-to-day life. He isn't my first psychiatrist. On my phone and calendar I call him Dr. P. My first was named Dr. C. Some part of me is still paranoid that someone will come across one of their full names in my phone or calendar and know my secret. I'm still not quite sure what happened; why, in my late thirties, did depression interrupt my life once again?

My fear—one of my biggest fears—is that it will happen, that it will happen again. Like in college, but worse. My early twenties were punctuated by two very serious depressions that led to me dropping out and moving and spending months repairing my sanity. But I have kids and a career and rent and student loans now. I have a relatively functional adult life. I just bought a minivan and took my kid to the doctor. I'm a fucking responsible adult now. I can't just drop out and run home to sleep and then travel until I feel better. My dad is dead and gone and my mom lives in a small apartment—nowhere to go. A part of me wants to grab the tent out of the garage and just live in the woods. I knew the perfect spot where no one would bother me. I'm starting to see why my estranged father had settled for that life. Life in the world is fucking hard. But that wasn't going to be my life. It isn't my life.

My worst fear is that I will get depressed and not be able to function. And it came true. It happened. It happened again. I lost my shit. It didn't happen the way I expected, but looking back maybe I should have known. With bipolar disorder, the higher up you get the bigger the crash when you come down. It sneaks up on you. My career was going great, I was working a lot, working a side hustle making a name for myself in my industry. Helping people. I had gotten in great shape from riding my bike a few years ago… but my waistline was starting to grow again. My marriage was under the modern strain of two working parents trying to be present to our jobs and our kids and ourselves and each other. We had a new baby who quickly became a spirited toddler, and my older daughter was diagnosed with an illness that required weekly visits to the outpatient clinic at the children's hospital. My grandfather died. No living father figures left.

I was stressed out. I could feel the black dog of depression darkening my door. My sense of humor was less enthusiastic, I was exhausted, irritable, not sleeping well, losing motivation to exercise. My psychiatrist, Dr. P, was in favor of changing my meds and I was coming around… after finally getting to a minimal amount of Lamictal, but never quite off, it was time to pile on more. We went down the menu of options…. I had already taken Wellbutrin, Zoloft, Paxil, Ambien, Carbamazepine, Lamictal, Gabapentin, Seroquel, Nefazodone, Lorazepam, Lithium, and a few others.

I came of age at the same time as psychopharmacology. Doctors had been tinkering and testing biological approaches to psychiatry in hospitals and private offices for decades, but by the late nineties Prozac was a blockbuster and psychiatric drugs were prescribed to the masses. They soon became a staple of primary care prescriptions. Paxil and Zoloft soon followed, my first two introductions to the little magic pills. By 2020 the pharmaceutical companies have created a menu of psychoactive drugs longer than the wine list at a fancy restaurant. It is big business, keeping people sane. As much as I suspect being just another victim of this pharmaceutical arms race, I have also accepted that these drugs have helped me. They are a necessary part of my life. Maybe if I had never started them I would have recovered on my own and never become dependent on them for survival. Maybe I would never have had to wrestle with a full-on diagnosis of "crazy." Maybe I would have created a healthy life on my own. Or maybe I would have deteriorated into mental illness, always treading water, if able to keep my head above water at all, alive at all. I carry these contradictions with me.

I have read the books—*Anatomy of an Epidemic* and many others. Psych meds are controversial for good reason. But I am a lifer. I have taken all the supplements: fish oil, vitamin D, B vitamins, kava kava, 5-HTP, probiotics, spirulina, melatonin, the list goes on. I still take some of them. They certainly help with my energy and balancing out my moods and overall health, but nothing compares to good old prescription drugs.

My life seems better on them than off, and I'm not willing to face the withdrawal anyway. I was willing to entertain what else the pharmacy had to offer… though sometimes it is tempting to pick something off the menu that you know is good, even if it makes you fat and tired.

I was reluctant to try something new. The reason why I wasn't still taking any of these medications anymore is because I didn't like the side effects, diarrhea, increased suicidal thoughts, brain fog, sluggishness, tremor, weight gain. But these were the devils I knew. Lithium stood apart from the others. Despite the tremor and the 75 pounds I gained, that shit worked. The lights came on a week after I started taking it. I was no longer sleeping with someone who wanted to kill me. I have no doubt that it saved my life. The path that led me to lithium started nearly twenty years ago.

Classical Psychiatry

I hated Dr. C, my first psychiatrist, before I even met him, and more after I did. He represented what I had been taught to question: emotional problems were to be dealt with by talking and love and romance and meditation and vitamins and diet and pursuing your dreams and finding your passions and higher education and working harder and vacations—not psychiatrists and their cabinets full of poison tablets and half-truths about the human mind.

I was a skeptic, to say the least, when I first darkened Dr. C's door. But I was desperate. I wanted to die. I had tried to die, and failed. More than once. And part of me wanted to live. There was still a little bit of hope.

I stepped off the city bus into a gray rainy northwest day. Underdressed in a hoodie and tennis shoes, I was soaked before I made it across the sidewalk. I checked the address that my dad had scribbled on an old envelope, feeling uncertain as this looked like a residential street. But the numbers matched what was on my paper. I stepped onto the porch. Next to the door was a sign with names followed by MD, PhD, PsyD, LMHC, and LICSW. It wasn't until much later in life that I could easily translate this alphabet soup. Dr. C, MD, Psychiatry. This was the place.

I stepped out of the miserable soggy day—not unlike how I felt inside—into a nicely-appointed waiting room. I distinctly remember that classical music was playing from a cheap clock radio. I'm not sure if that is a trick they learn in medical school, that classical music is equal to white noise and much more pleasant than those loud ocean churning machines. Dr. P's lobby plays the same station. Private conversations are happening nearby. This is not a place you want to be overheard.

I've learned in my life that bravery and courage are not about the absence of fear, but the acceptance of doing something that is necessary despite the terror it evokes and emotional or physical risk it could lead to. It is worth facing the pain because it is important. You also may not have any other choice. Out of options. All roads had led me here. There was no escaping this appointment, this meeting with destiny; but not the kind of destiny you imagine with love or vocation; it is the hard stuff that is part of your life, no matter what.

I have come to understand that this is my inheritance. This meeting with my psychiatrist was not dissimilar to being summoned to an estate attorney's office to learn that you have inherited great wealth from a long-lost uncle or estranged father. Except this inheritance wouldn't buy me houses or cars or happiness. The genetics of mental illness remain complicated and mysterious, but one thing is very clear: it is passed on from one generation to the next.

I picked up a magazine and pretended to read it. I was alone in this waiting room, or was I? It was me and Chopin and a year's worth of *People* magazines. My neck, barely covered by my oversized hooded sweatshirt, still burned from the rope of my own private gallows, the one I barely escaped alive from. I rub the faint scar on my wrist that was treated at the ER in my college town a few years ago. My memory drifts back to that terrible night in the bathtub and the events that led up to it. I never want to go back to that college town.

My reverie on my past and simultaneous deep dive into celebrity heartbreak, with a classical backing track, was interrupted as I heard a door creak, down a hallway I couldn't see. A woman soon walked through the doorway into the lobby, rubbing her eyes with a Kleenex, holding a square of white paper. We avoided eye contact and then she was gone. On her heels was a tall slender man in a sweater. He had round glasses, bald, save cropped white hair above his ears.

His sharp blue eyes looked in my direction; I could already feel him evaluating me, examining my every movement, analyzing my childhood and preparing to tattoo "crazy" on my forehead. Judging me. I hated him. "███," he said with a gentle smile. I nodded and meekly got up, dropping my magazine on the coffee table as he motioned me to follow him down the hall. I took a deep breath—this was a moment of courage — despite so much of me wanting to run back into the wet gray uncertainty of the winter.

I shuffled behind Dr. C and he motioned for me to sit on a blue velvet couch as he settled into a solid wood rocking chair and set a yellow pad and pen on his lap. I handed him the paperwork he had mailed and I had completed, the only homework that this soon-to-be college dropout had finished all quarter. I honestly don't remember much from that first meeting, besides the hating him and the self-loathing and the suspicion and the desperation, clinging to the hope that this polite but stern man in this simple room might be my savior. I left with my own square of white paper and a sample pack of blue pills. I boarded the bus, hope in my pocket but feeling that somehow I had deeply betrayed some code that I had agreed to abide by, the code that set me and my people apart from the rest that were lazy and slothful and escaped from their problems with pills instead of facing them and solving them.

I felt humiliated, but I was alive and I had a new plan besides suicide. I was going to take these pills. As prescribed, one a day until I felt better. The blue pills had some effect, but I was still struggling, and after a few misses and trials of other medicines, Dr C suggested what sounded to me like the nuclear option. Lithium. He handed me a research study on it, as an adjunct treatment to antidepressants. At that point he didn't think I was bipolar, just depressed— but there was a good chance this would help. It said so in the study anyway.

But wasn't lithium what they gave the really really crazy people? Like the Joker and the rest at Arkham Asylum? I had always aspired to act more like Bruce Wayne and Batman, and I doubted they were taking any lithium. They had found other ways to battle their demons. But I was desperate, so I agreed.

I had to get regular blood tests, every time a bit nervous that the latest result would show that my kidney function was destroyed. My mild shakiness turned into a full-on tremor, my hands sometimes shaking like a maple leaf in the breeze. My hunger was ravenous.

But I felt better. A lot better. A light switch flipped. I woke up a week later in the bed I had been spending most of my time in, plotting my death, and wanted to live. I really wanted to live. I wanted to do things and go outside and be a human again. My life was still a wreck, but I wasn't so stuck in rumination that I couldn't get back to the business of living. Instead of lying in bed awake all night thinking about how I would never amount to anything and would never get a job, I looked for a job. I got a job and then a year later a better job. I finished college. I finished graduate school. The girl that visited me when I was so sad—she and I got married and had babies. I had a life. I had the life that I wanted so bad and was afraid I would never have. That is still my life.

My depression has ebbed and flowed since I first met Dr. C, but has never been so bad again that it disrupted the structure of my life. It was really hard to say goodbye when he retired. He really helped me. Since I sought psychiatric care there has been no more dropping out. I have been steadily employed, steadily married, steady, stable for almost 20 years. I've taken some breaks, sure, but those were commas that let me stop and take a breath, rather than new chapters starting life from scratch. I've been under the care of a psychiatrist since I was 22 years old. My fear is that that black dog will come back to finish what he started, sedated in the corner where I keep him at bay—but he awakes often enough to remind me he is still there. He usually just pins me to the floor or the wall in despair or chases me with a fierce anxiety that shakes me to the core, but he has stopped plotting to kill me—for now.

The memories from that time haunt me. I was so broken. But finally the dark thoughts cleared and I was ok again. Before long I was rolling burritos at a local taco shop and getting more serious with my girlfriend. She was a sucker for my big sad eyes. I talked her into moving to up to the big city. When the lease came up for renewal, I moved into her apartment, and Dad and my brother moved out too. They later moved to California. I filled a hotel room with rose petals and popped the question. She said yes. I had a good management job in human services and was back in school. I had an internship lined up. I was able to finish my degree without going back to campus. I was relieved. Back on track. Things were going well. I had also gained a lot of weight. I was struggling to balance the side effects of my medication with the newfound stability of my biochemistry. I stopped lithium and tried a lot of other medications, most consistently Lamictal. It dulled me, slowed my brain down a little bit, but seemed to manage my depression pretty well. I lost weight. I hated being fat even more than I hated feeling dumb. But most of all I liked being alive.

Refill

But all these years later, before I even considered the day hospital, lithium was on the menu again. When Dr. P, my current psychiatrist, goes through the list of my medications, rather than opening what seemed like a scarier box, the antipsychotics for depression like Latuda or Abilify, I opted to try what I knew worked: lithium - shake weight be damned.

The pharmacist asked me if this was a new prescription and I shook my head gently and said "No, I've taken it before." I sat in the front seat of my car and stared at the yellow bottle with the white label for what felt like an eternity. I distinctly remember picking up the prescription, looking at the bottle and thinking "Hello lithium, my old friend."

I never thought we'd be back together. I had ended our relationship years before, but now here we are again. I pushed down on the child safe cap and opened it, pouring more than I needed into my hand. The small capsules were kind of cute, dark pink like the color of my daughter's baby doll, and shiny too. Certainly not as terrifying as a nuclear torpedo. Maybe I can win the war again. I pour the lion's share back in the bottle and am left with one sparkling sphere. I throw it down the hatch and take a pull from my metal water bottle. We're doing this.

The lithium didn't work so dramatically this time. It wasn't clear if it was helping, but it was clear that I was still struggling. No light switches flipped. But I was still trying to keep up a crazy pace—my highly visible project at work was launching and going well but all consuming, my wife and daughters needed a lot of attention, and the healthy diet and exercise routine that had helped me to better manage my weight and mood was slipping. I rode my bike less and less. It felt like I was struggling to hold up the weight of the world and it was threatening to crush me. I had to keep going, I couldn't slow down, I couldn't be that lost boy in the rain with rope burn on his neck. I was someone else now. I had so much to lose. I had to keep going. And then I couldn't. I was exhausted, out of gas.

The suicidal thoughts started to come around again. They are seductive. It isn't so much a big dark thought at first. Your mind is searching for solutions, something is wrong, there is pain. Our minds like to solve problems. When the list of solutions seems exhausted, when you've looked in all the doors and come up empty, there is one more door. It is painted black. It is a closet full of rope and pills and maps to bridges without guardrails.

I would go about my day, often distracted, but in my quieter moments, or when my mind wandered, I would more and more often entertain the solutions offered behind that dark door. It is a relief to feel like there is a way out, the way you are driving and have to pee but relax when you see a sign for a rest stop, even if it is a few miles off. I needed an off-ramp, and I was running out of options that my mind would accept.

One problem with depression is that my mind often gets stuck in black and white or all-or-nothing thinking. My field of vision becomes narrow and I lose perspective on what other options might exist for help. My psychiatrist and I had been talking about me taking a leave from work but I was ambivalent, and so was he. We agreed that I shouldn't just sit alone at home for extended periods. Netflix, it turns out, is not an evidence-based treatment for depression. I also didn't need to be hospitalized. I had suicidal thoughts but no intention of acting on them. Yet. That was what terrified me.

I have had suicidal thoughts on and off for my entire adult life. They are usually fleeting, and certainly not constant. But there are occasions that they've hijacked the narrative of my brain. And once upon a time I did act on them; they consumed me, and I had to act. At the time it didn't feel like I had a choice. It was not a question of if I would kill myself, only when. I was terrified that I was on that road again. That is why I went to the day hospital.

Number Two

A few years into treatment with Dr. C, he suggested that I might consider another diagnosis. There was emerging literature on bipolar II disorder, and the cases and symptoms described sounded a lot like me. Antidepressants alone had made me worse, mood stabilizers had made me better. As more and more people were taking SSRIs, or antidepressants, they were finding that a subset experienced medication-induced mania or dangerous suicidality. Those patients better responded to bipolar medications, and often their diagnosis was adjusted.

Part of the challenge with the treatment of this disorder is that people often don't seek care when they're manic or hypomanic—unless psychosis or risky behavior catch the attention of family or law enforcement. People experiencing mania are feeling pretty good, maybe too good, but they certainly don't have time or any reason to go to the doctor. There are a thousand more important things to do. But then the crash comes and we get so depressed, so down, few would suspect the high energy ball of fire that just burned out. Doctors don't see the manic part and they treat only the depression. They don't always screen for mania, or they don't ask the questions that would tell the other part of the story. So we are treated solely for depression and things get worse. People with bipolar disorder are at higher risk for suicide than people with major depression alone. This is part of the reason.

Psychiatrists and clinical social workers and other mental health professionals are trained to look closely for the hidden past of bipolar disorder, but many general practitioners aren't. Family history is a good indicator, but some families never talk about it, or some are never treated so never diagnosed. Maybe an uncle that drank a lot and flew off the handle and then disappeared into the basement for weeks at a time, or the distant aunt that was in a mental institution for some unknown reason. An estranged sibling that had struggled to launch and now took some unknown medications. In my case it was both of my grandmothers, my mother, my father, my brother, and me. As far as someone with bipolar disorder goes, my official diagnosis is modified with "mild"; some might call me high-functioning. But I am uncomfortable with the high-functioning label, as much as I appreciate its effort to pull me away from the ranks of the truly insane or permanently disabled. Sometimes I am barely functioning at all.

High-Functioning

Earlier in my career I spent a lot of time with people with intellectual and developmental disabilities. Some had severe autism. I'm talking the nonverbal, repetitive motion, restricted hobbies, totally dependent on others, behaviorally challenging, and often very very sweet type of autism. I have many dear friends who have or have children with this condition, and as hard as it can be, there are many blessings.

Later in my career I spent more time with people with Asperger's syndrome, a diagnosis that was recently scrapped in favor of broadening the autism spectrum. Some people refer to these folks as "high-functioning." They can sometimes pass as "normal," or "typical" as people in the disability community prefer to call the normies. But these folks really struggle in social situations, in relationships, at work, are easily overstimulated, and have restricted interests that are often considered odd or overly intense. I have known many non-verbal people who were called "low-functioning," who had social and intellectual skills superior to those that could talk your ear off about astrophysics. They often endured vicious bullying as children for these differences, bullying that sometimes continues in their adult life, though more manifested by isolation and peers leaving them out because they don't fit in. Sometimes their symptoms get more intense and it becomes hard to function. It is hard enough to be a relatively functional adult in this world without a disability. "High-functioning" is a myth that I am happy to hide behind. Except that I am terrified of being found out as really just "good at pretending." I am afraid that I am one bad depressive episode away from long-term disability. High-functioning indeed.

Loss

I was recently at the park with my friend and our kids. He is a successful guy who works for a big tech company. He had done theatre with my wife in college before he started writing music for video games and then managing complex technology projects. He was telling me the details of his father's recent suicide. Sadness welled up in my throat, memories of a few years before when I discovered my own father's corpse, a life cut short by heart disease. This was Dad, ██████████, the one that had raised me. The coroner had ruled his death a heart attack. He died alone so no one quite knew what his last moments were like. As far as I can tell he was winded from carrying boxes up four flights of stairs and sat down and then laid down for a nap that lasted three days, until we found him.

I thought of my cousin and aunt, a few years before that, who also left through that dark door of suicide. The moment my friend started sharing, I just wanted to numb out, stop feeling, and intellectualize it all. The wash of painful memories and their accompanying emotions were too much to bear. Yet I recently committed to no longer run from or block these feelings, and I value being present to my friend, so I pulled my attention back from the black cloud of the past and into the present moment. My friend's father had walked into the backyard and shot himself in the head in front of his wife, my friend's mother. It was tragic and horrifying and so very very sad. As much as I had worked in my life to keep myself and others from this tragic fate, it is still happening. It happens every day, and the numbers are trending up. As my mind chattered on in the background, trying to solve suicide, trying to figure out my next move in the Sisyphean battle to cure human suffering, I realized that I was keeping my emotional distance. I took a deep breath and turned my full attention to my friend as he wept, my hand on his shoulder. I shivered with the pain of his loss and the visceral memories of those that I have lost. Grief never ends, but over time the intensity may decline. I don't want to stop grieving those that I have lost. I loved them that much.

We watched our children play. Their paternal grandfathers would only be known to them through stories. Still young men, in our thirties, feeling too young to be adrift without the guidance of these men who had once held us when we slept and disciplined us when we misbehaved. Both of our fathers died of preventable heart problems, but as difficult as it was, my father's end wasn't so tragic. I imagine that he had chest pains and laid down and drifted off to sleep. He had expected to wake up, he had wanted to. That moment in his life was marked with hope and possibility and positivity. His funeral was not clouded by the shame that he had done something terribly wrong, beyond being more vigilant about his cholesterol.

We shepherded our children into car seats and hugged and slapped each other on the back. "Hang in there," I said, "let me know if there is anything I can do to help." I worried he was depressed too. He was grieving and that is natural, I just didn't want my dear friend to slip into the black hole that I and his father had been caught in. Not all of us get out alive. Later, things did get darker for him, but he got good professional help, and he is thriving now.

Exhaustion

A couple of months after I left the day hospital, Dr. P and I decided that I should go off my Lithium. The Prozac seems to have been what lifted my depression and I'm still taking Lamictal for mood stabilization. I'm not depressed, but I'm exhausted. I'm sleeping all the time. I've watched 4 seasons of *NYPD Blue* in two weeks. I'm back at work but slacking off in all of my downtime and I know that my lack of enthusiasm isn't sustainable. My wife is doing the lion's share around the house, tending to the children, shopping, and cleaning. I have started to cook again and am trying to help with what I can, but it's hard to keep my eyes open. My default is to sleep — and I am a guy that usually has a lot of trouble sleeping.

During my time at the day hospital I was depleted emotionally and titrating up on medications—a good recipe for fatigue. I was in bed by 7 or 8 every night and slept until 7 the next morning. In my typical routine I usually struggle to be in bed before midnight. We increased my lithium then, at the urging of the psychiatrist at the day hospital. My suicidal thoughts were troublesome and another 300mg might turn down the volume. The Prozac hadn't kicked in yet.

It was as much my idea as the doctor's. It seemed reasonable to be tired then, in early November, and even during the week I took off for Thanksgiving. That was a really intense time, I chalked up my exhaustion to needing to slow down and continue the reboot I had started at the day hospital. But then we went away for Christmas, away from our routine of required activities. And I slept. No matter what time, I went to sleep, usually early, I would sleep until around noon. My wife and kids were busy with my in-laws, but they all did wonder about me. I was pleasant and engaged in the afternoons…and then I would nap, have dinner, watch a movie, and go to sleep again. It was fine for vacation, but not sustainable.

A couple weeks into the New Year, I slept in on the weekend. I woke up at 11 to my wife stressing about the to-do list for the day. I picked a few things and got them done, but feeling the tension I went downstairs and sought distraction on my phone. Drowsy, I dropped the phone and fell asleep. I just wanted to sleep. Probably shouldn't, but ohhh, it feels so good to just sleep and sleep and sleep. Once again I was seduced into slumber.

She found me asleep, registered her dissatisfaction with a huff, and left. I crawled into the guest bed nearby and slept the rest of the afternoon. She later came down, as patiently as she could and asked if I was just going to sleep or if I was still planning to go along for our evening plans. "Of course," I said, acting offended at the thought that I wouldn't. I showered and woke up and we had a perfectly pleasant evening. My mom was watching the kids and we had the chance for a rare dinner date. I could still feel the tension from our earlier exchange but she didn't show it. A picture of loveliness, dolled up for a night out with her man. She ordered wine and I ordered soda.

The psychiatrist at the day hospital had recommended that I avoid alcohol for six months, even though it wasn't a big concern for me. It was fine, I could take it or leave it. I don't drink very often, but looking back I had recognized a trend of occasional binge drinking (I like to party) that I best avoid in my current condition. As long as I could still eat steak and chocolate, my key vices were still intact.

During dinner the concern about my oversleeping came up. She said "all you do is sleep and watch TV." I acknowledged that that was mostly true, but that I had been cooking more, that I had been playing with the kids, taking them to school; I was doing a lot more than I had been a month ago. I was really trying. I wiped tears from my eyes. But she was right. I was far from functioning at full capacity. I was comfortably numb. This hibernation had maybe been necessary to level me out, but it was not sustainable.

I called Dr. P the next day. He agreed that the lithium was doing more harm than good. He gave me instructions for tapering off of it. Drop a pill every week or so and be off it completely in 4-6 weeks. I was hopeful. I had gained 30 pounds and was feeling apathetic about doing anything involving sweat. My mojo, my spark, still wasn't back. I wasn't depressed. I was just "fine," but I wanted to be better than fine, I wanted to be good, to be great.

About three weeks after I started tapering the lithium I noticed that my energy was returning. Some nights I didn't sleep as well, especially soon after I dropped the dose, but it seemed to even out. Even when I didn't sleep well I had a lot more energy during the day. My mood was still good. Not depressed. There were about 10 more capsules of lithium in the bottle. Shiny little pink magic salt shakers. I could have stopped and left them in the bottle. It had been a week since I dropped the dose last. But I didn't sleep well that night and I was still nervous about letting go. But whether it was that night or the next week, I planned to take the last pill and not refill the prescription. This companion that came to stay for a year would be out of the house once again. I considered leaving the following note in the bottle when I threw it in the trash:

You didn't cure me this time, but I needed you, I needed to finish what we started. I needed to calm my nerves, I needed to rest and remember what was important, I needed to put my feet back on the ground. I needed to hibernate for a while. I needed to stop hating you and accept that it is ok that you were once a part of my life and may be again. I am not broken. I am human. Sometimes even humans need a little help to get put back together. The cast is coming off. Thank you for your healing power. Until we meet again.

Goodbye lithium, my old friend.

Follow-up

Wait, wait, wait… hold the phone!!! My poetic ending took a turn. In my last few days on that lowest dose of lithium my mood, which had been dramatically improving, heated up. My mood was really, really good. Too good. I wrote most of this book in a week after barely writing for years. I bought a new car. I spent a lot of money. I had a million thoughts about a million things. I was talking faster and feeling pressured and tight in my bones. I was irritable and snappy and defensive at home. I thought up a c-suite promotion for myself and almost sent the half-baked proposal to the CEO before being backed off the ledge by a diplomatic peer. I wasn't sleeping or exercising much, but I had more energy than I could remember ever having in recent years.

My spark wasn't just back, I was on fire. I was hilarious again. My social media feeds blew up with awesome posts. Is this what it feels like to not be depressed, or is this something else? I was louder at work, what started as flirtatious charm and boisterous humor turned into biting sarcasm and an intensity that seemed to put people on their heels. I was interrupting people a lot. What happened to the sleepy friendly fellow in the corner? I remember this quizzical look that a coworker, a former marine, gave me. It was like he knew something was off and was concerned, or maybe protective of everyone else around me. Was the scary monster coming out?

My wife expressed concern that I was a bit "up." I had finally ridden my bike to work that week, had seen a private practice client again—this was the week I was supposed to be officially recovered. I had one more lithium pill left. "Up?" Damn, I knew she was right. In our vocabulary "up" is a subtle way of saying "hypomanic."

If my mindfulness practice has given me anything, it is the ability to step back and notice what is going on for me emotionally and cognitively. I couldn't turn it off, but I could notice it. My feelings and my thoughts and my body were running hot for sure. Compared to how I had been feeling, this was amazing, but I was starting to overheat. I agreed that I needed to get it checked out. I got in to see Dr. P the next day. I told him everything in one energetic run-on sentence. He looked at me with fascination. I had been a lethargic lump, an Eeyore just a month before, and now I was Tigger incarnate, talking fast and describing all of the great things I was doing and the problems they were starting to cause. He confirmed what I knew. I was hypomanic and I was headed in the direction of mania. He was concerned that if we didn't make a change now, find a way to give me a soft landing, the crash would be dark and dangerous. He cut my Prozac dose in half, in case that was contributing, and had me double up on the lithium. He cautioned me to avoid behavior that had gotten me in trouble in the past.

My wife had come with me to the appointment. She and our younger daughter waited in the lobby with the classical music. At the end I brought her into the office to hear about the plan. I was relieved that she could be in the room that I always talked about but she had never entered. My run-on sentence continued to interrupt as Dr. P shared the plan with my wife. She is an important part of my care team and I was glad they could connect. On the way out I reached into my jacket pocket and pulled out my lithium bottle…there was one more pill… it was supposed to be my last. I filled a paper cup at the water cooler and popped the shiny pink magic pill into my mouth. Down the hatch.

Well lithium, my old friend, make yourself comfortable. It looks like you're going to be here for a while.

Better

Within a couple of days I was sleeping better and feeling more balanced. I still had energy in the mornings and was productive at work, but not so edgy, not so intense, not so pressured. I was ok, felt pretty good actually. I asked for a promotion that was reasonable, not five steps above my pay grade. I didn't crash or overheat…things just smoothed out. We took a road trip in the "funny van" as our toddler calls it. In my hypomania I had bought a minivan; there are worse sins. I was glad I had the lithium on board. I guess it was doing something after all. I'm glad to be alive.

12

Oh Brother, Where Art Thou?

Not long after the medication from my first psychiatrist, Dr. C, started working, I was ready to get back to my life. When I moved out of that halfway house at my dad's and in with my girlfriend, my brother went to live with friends. It seemed like a good idea at the time. Soon we became aware that they were all using crystal meth, but that was only one of the concerns. His meth-using friends kicked him out because of how strange he was acting. I wish I had been paying more attention. He wasn't well. It was easy to blame the drugs, his weak will, his inability to take responsibility for his life, but he was struggling with something deeper, something not entirely in his own control. The terror that is my mental illness pales in comparison to what he has been through with his. He became homeless.

Later, my dad got a job in California and my brother went down too, no other options I guess. My brother's mental health continued to deteriorate and he was homeless for some time. He eventually got into a group home and later moved back home to public housing in our hometown. Not much has changed since he came back. He smokes filterless cigarettes and mutters to himself and is relatively pleasant, but he is a shell of the beautiful outgoing boy I spent my childhood with.

A few years before we all lived in that halfway house, my brother ran away. I was in college. He was still in high school, though on the verge of dropping out. I reached out to everyone I knew, that he knew. He had burned a lot of bridges. When I found him his speech was rapid and his eyes were dilated. He swore up and down that he was clean – that the meth, marijuana, and other untold self-medications were behind him. He refused to consider professional help.

The inpatient psychiatric hospital that he had been committed to earlier in the year was not something he would ever return to willingly. It was traumatizing and humiliating—but he didn't recognize the trauma and humiliation that his psychotic episode and ongoing instability had caused for him and for our family. He was angry and suspicious. He refused to come home with me.

The next time I saw him he was behind thick glass in an orange jumpsuit. The delusions had finally caught up with him; he had burned all his bridges, and at that point only the criminal justice system could slow down his self-destructive spiral.

My childhood playmate, my rowdy companion: my brother and I shared big dreams of the future. He was the strong one—always sticking up for me, chasing away the bullies that antagonized me. But I was the big brother, the one who was supposed to protect him. And then one day we were teenagers, and he started to fade away. I don't know how I missed it—too self-absorbed with my own survival to notice, I guess, but one day that bright, blue-eyed boy was gone.

He is "ok" and "stable" now; the nightmare is over. I no longer worry that the next call will be from the jailer, or worse, the coroner. He is sober, with a diagnosis, a prescription, and a disability check. Months of homelessness and a string of petty crimes finally qualified him for the support he needed. These days he is lucid enough to carry on a short conversation before spacing off to who knows where, or talking quietly to everyone but the people in the room. I hope that someday we will be best friends again, confiding secrets and dreams, but for now, I am happy just to know where he is.

Firewood

Many autumns ago my mom asked us to go out into her back yard and stack the cord of wood she had just had delivered in a pickup truck by a guy I went to high school with. Mom always puts her boys to work when they come around. This particular chore was one we were glad to fulfill, as it was once an arduous task, but now a reminder of simpler times.

The crisp air washed over my face with the fresh reminder of fall. Suddenly I was in a moment of timeless memory. There was a pile of wood to be stacked and my brother and I were not allowed to escape to the warmth of the indoors until it was carried and neatly organized. My forearms began to ache as my sweatshirt took on the red hue of bark and leaves. My brother and I worked silently, each lost in our own worlds. We have a system down. We throw the wood close to the house and then stack it up. He takes periodic breaks to smoke and mutter to himself, while I continue to work. The pile does not seem to get any smaller, but I know if we keep moving it will go away eventually.

It strikes me that it has been a long time since I've done this chore, yet it is so very familiar. It was another house in the woods where so much wood was stacked. Dad would go out on our land and fell big old trees and cut them into rounds with his chainsaw. Stacked under blue tarps, they dried during the summer, creating a home for spiders and other insects. When the days began to get shorter we would pull on our old tennis shoes and ratty jeans and sharpen the axes. We'd roll back the blue tarps and find a sturdy round to use as a chopping block and wail away. A victimless pursuit, these long-dead trees offered an outlet for the angst of adolescence and the anger of youth.

Timeless, I think as I carefully add to the stack, reminded of many unremarkable moments such as this that take me back to a predictable routine in an unpredictable childhood. When I was a little boy my dad quit a good job in California and moved his family to the Pacific Northwest. He had enough saved to buy ten acres in the woods and build a home for his family. Back then it was just me and my older brother, but within a few years there were two more redheaded boys, the "red riot" as my dad affectionately called us. He built a big cedar house on that land, heated by a single wood stove. As soon as we were big enough to carry a stick of wood we were enlisted, and before long we each had mastered the finer points of swinging an axe.

Even after Mom took us and left and Dad remarried and we only came over a couple of weekends a month, we were still expected to keep the mud room full of wood. I now long for the familiarity of this chore. Things were simpler then, the possibilities endless. Our oldest and youngest brothers spent time on the bookends with each of us, but somehow it is this brother that I most remember spending many long hours laboring out there with, talking about our dreams for the future – the beautiful women we would marry and the millions we would have and the Ferraris we would drive. We would vacillate between such grandiose talk and petty brotherly arguments and long stretches of silence. In the silence we each carried our own internal dialogue, and as time passed, it so often, for me anyway, was spent scheming the possibilities for what I would do when I finally escaped the indentured servitude of the wood pile.

And here we are so many years later, more lost in our own worlds than ever. I, thinking about where my career will go in a few months after I complete graduate school, of the terror and excitement of impending fatherhood, and feeling the weight of sadness at the neverending loss of my brother. He is standing right there, smoking a cigarette and gesturing into thin air. He is having an intense discussion with an invisible man, so much so that he has very little left to say to me or anyone else in the material world.

At this moment I wish that this pile of wood was not already cut and that I had an axe and rounds to split. The rage bubbling up inside of me is palpable. I am furious at him, at my parents, at the system, and most of all myself. Somewhere along the line I failed him as an older brother, too occupied by my own dreams to notice that my brother was slipping away. He takes medication that seems to calm his wild streak, but does not seem to do much to dampen his rich fantasy life. He has never spoken to me about his mental illness. He may never come back, and will definitely never be the boy that I miss so much.

We each carry our final load to our neatly stacked pile. Another round of this chore is complete. "Ready to go in for dinner?" I ask. "Yeah sure, but I'm going to stay out here a minute." I shrug my shoulders and pat him on the shoulder as he lights up another cigarette and resumes his muted conversation with the invisible man. I slip inside, into the warm arms of my pregnant wife.

Not much has changed since that day. The child who grew in my wife's belly just celebrated her eighth birthday, and now she has a little sister. We see my brother every month or two. My kids call him Uncle ████, but I get the sense that they're a little confused by him. I wonder when the right time is to tell a kid that her uncle has schizoaffective disorder, and for that matter that her father and his father have its less psychotic sibling, bipolar disorder. How do you explain genetic predisposition, that there is a chance that she might be crazy too? That conversation is for another day; for now she knows that Dad takes a lot of vitamins and has a feelings doctor that he talks to.

Hope

My mom recently took over as my brother's Medicaid caregiver. After some urging she talked him into going to the dentist. They pulled 10 teeth. She got him a toothbrush and helped him clean his apartment. They found a case manager that he liked. They shopped for healthier food. He agreed to see a psychiatrist. Whatever meds he had been taking, the prescription had run out years ago. He was talking to himself a lot and not able to focus on much, behavior I had come to accept as his baseline. But he agreed to go to the psychiatrist. He started a new medication. I kind of forgot about it, honestly.

He came over to my house last weekend. He was quiet but not talking to an unseen being. He wasn't smoking as much. We watched a movie and I brought him all the snacks I could muster up. He was hungry. I wondered if he had eaten yet that day. We had just filled our cupboards at Costco. I really wanted to feed him.

He pushed my toddler daughter in her stroller when we went up to the park. She is so lovely and engaging; she is happy to love anyone I love. She could tell how much I love my brother. He pushed her on the swing. That park was the last place I ever saw our dad. As my brother gets older, his hair thinning, his waistline broadening, those sparkling blue eyes and wide smile and that Sicilian silhouette, he looks so much like him. Unmistakable who his father is.

I finally pried my daughter out of the baby swing and my brother pushed her in the stroller again. We went to a coffee shop and read a story together. I could see that it was hard for him to concentrate, but he was really trying. It was at that moment that I noticed the change. Subtle, but definitely better… he was better!

Dare I hope that he will emerge, that maybe there will be more to his life than what I had settled for in my acceptance of his illness, of his refusal to accept help? I don't know. I don't dare get my hopes up for more than this. But he is reading a story to his niece. His voice has the timbre of his father's, of our dad's. I wipe a tear from my eye. I'm glad he is in my children's lives. I'm glad he is in my life.

13

Invisible Disability

Diversity

I once thought of my life as a profound journey toward self-realization and understanding. Pain was understood to be part of the price of admission to experiencing infinite love. The world was full of peril; anything mainstream was questioned. Incense, meditation, and new-age philosophy permeated my childhood home. I no longer feel that way.

I'm an average guy. Not necessarily boring or lame or anything like that, but I strive to be typical, in the best sense of the word. I fly under the radar. My style tends toward the unassuming; I prefer to blend in, rather than stand out. I don't have tattoos or piercings. I keep my hair short. I'm respectful toward everyone I meet. I'm not an asshole. I'm a really nice guy. For years my preferred colors were dark browns, greens, grays, and black. Perfect shades for blending into the Pacific Northwest backdrop that has always been my home. I am married, have kids, and have been steadily employed for my whole adult life. I have debt. I drive a late model Toyota. I am normal.

I strive for a typical existence. Extraordinary lives are overrated. I went to college, survived graduate school, and have a few letters after the name on my business card. My identity as a white, straight, cisgender man with a middle-class pedigree is worn like protective armor. It is only in recent years that I have come to understand what powerful armor this is. I cling tightly to it, especially when my disability flares and the privileges it affords me feel at risk.

Until I was awakened to the reality of my white privilege, I felt like most white guys who are scrapping to survive in this world. When proposals are made to even the playing field and roll back our special privileges, we get defensive because it doesn't feel like we have any. We haven't noticed those who don't look like us that are trailing behind us. We are too busy trying to keep up with the white men with a wide lead ahead of us. The world of men is bitterly competitive, and if we don't keep up we will lose. We will suffer. We might die. Our families will starve. Losing is not an option. We weren't raised to compete with women or minorities. We were raised to compete with other white men. We don't feel like we're winning. But we are. We wrestle in a rarefied arena that others are struggling to even get access to.

But the competition in this arena is fierce. There is always another guy with more money, smarts, strength, athleticism, virility, focus, the list goes on. We grew up losing to these guys. The battlefield of men is brutal. Some of us have retreated into female-dominated professions: social work, teaching, and nursing, and often rise to the top. We were raised to be leaders. We didn't notice those clawing behind us to survive, we were too focused on keeping up with the guy beating us up ahead. Laws that force structural equality may never quite balance the scales. The historical and cultural underpinnings of patriarchy are tough to overcome. The masculine drive for competition is intense. But so are the women that raised me and that are working with me and raising children alongside me. I want to raise my daughters to succeed in whatever they choose to pursue, and I hope I can model for them what success looks like and support their mother to do the same. I am surrounded by a diverse cast of characters at home and at work. My success is bound up with theirs. I wouldn't want it any other way. I want to win together.

Intersectionality

In graduate school I studied identity and intersectionality. I learned that who we are is inherited but also self-defined. We can choose, but many things are chosen for us: the community we grow up in, who our parents are, the color of our skin. I learned what I had been experiencing for most of my life, often unknowingly—that my anatomy and skin color give me a much different experience of the world than those without those attributes. When I found out that my father wasn't my father, my immature identity was in a tailspin. Everything was in doubt except for one thing: I was a white soon-to-be man. This current challenge to my identity didn't affect my whiteness or my maleness. My secret long-lost father wasn't black, or the secret would have been out years ago and I would have always known I was different.

███████, like ███████, is a solid American name. No one questions the country on my passport. The ███████, however, did a few generations ago change it from the Italian "███████", when my great-grandfather was looking for work and was denied it, until he took this step toward assimilation. He had to say goodbye to a name his family had passed on to their children for centuries. Forever after, in this country anyway, his descendants were the ███████.

This sacrifice has benefitted my uncles and my brothers and me immeasurably; no one ever questions that we are white American men. Our first names all came from the Bible. The American Dream is within reach for us.

I digress to this discussion on privilege, a sociological tangent, a rabbit hole of social justice that deserves no end of attention, not to shift focus to it entirely, but to acknowledge that despite my struggles with identity and disability, I am able to hide behind my whiteness and maleness and be well-compensated for it.

Part of the terror of my disease, of having a serious mental illness, is that I have so much to lose. I once had a boss tell me that I was the sanest person she knew. I chuckled on the outside but bristled internally; if only she knew the diagnoses on my medical chart or the heavy-duty medications flowing through my veins. If she only knew how much energy it took to keep up this facade on a bad day or week or month. I thought I gave up acting in high school. But the truth is that I have been an actor every day since. I've been promoted in every job I've ever had. I am surviving in an expensive city where to be middle-class you have to have two incomes each nearing six figures. My wife and children and I have plenty to eat, despite our occasional anxieties about paying the rent. Would this comfortable life be mine if my father was a black man or if my mental illness was more severe or not kept a secret? Probably not. It's not that I would not have been resilient and found my place as a person of color in a society stacked against me, but the odds are in the favor of the white boys that turn into white men.

This is part of the secret shame of stigma. I live as someone with an invisible disability. I have the choice, most of the time, to keep it secret, and that is to my benefit. On the job application for my current employer it asked, "Do you have a disability?"

with a list of examples including major depression and bipolar disorder. The choices: yes, no, prefer not to answer. In the past I had always checked "no," but this time I bravely checked "prefer not to answer." That was terrifying enough. No one ever asked me about it.

"You are the sanest person I know," that former boss said to me. Others have said as much. It is exhausting to keep up the charade, but necessary to ensure continued promotions and clothes for my children and food to eat and visits to the doctor and pills to keep me sane. I have heard from my black friends and colleagues of confusing times when people treat them poorly, and trying to discern whether it is bad manners or mood or a deeper animosity toward the color of their skin. As a white man, that is a question I never have to ask myself. Sometimes people are assholes—but not because of the color of my skin. Sometimes I get turned down for a job that I am well qualified for—but not because of the color of my skin.

Discrimination is not something I have to worry about. That is, except when my disability is no longer a secret. I worry when applying for roles with more responsibility and visibility, that my stability or competence might be called into question. This might not be explicit, I might not get the job for other reasons, but I will wonder. Would the interviewers knowing that I have a disability lead to some bias, even unconscious, against choosing me for the job? Or, do they know me, my work, my track record, and respect my struggle and honesty? I'm not sure how it will shake out if I make this public. Probably a bit of both. Is it worth the risk? Will I regret taking it, or regret not taking it? Ask me in 30 years and I'll tell you.

Electric Bike

I rode my bike to the pharmacy today. My prescription bottle for fluoxetine, or generic Prozac, was empty. The fancy transition lenses on my new glasses turned dark as I stepped into the sun and zipped on my bright orange waterproof jacket. It's not wet today but it's the beginning of February—cold, in the 40s.

The sun is out, so I have no excuse for not riding my bike to run errands, or at least my wife said as much. This jacket helps shield me from the wind that picks up when I pedal hard.

This bike is fast. 25 mph in a school zone fast. It is an electric, or e-bike. It has a Yamaha motor, like my first two motorcycles. My e-bike is black and green and German, like the BMW motorbike that I traded in when I quit my job and headed to graduate school.

I hope I never go full-on manic, because they would probably sell me a high performance vehicle that I would drive right off the lot. Wait, did I mention that I once bought a brand new BMW motorcycle when I was making about $30k per year? They just let me have the keys. I was amazed. And I paid it off, never laid it down. But I got lots of speeding tickets.

I rode it all the way to Utah and let it out in the Bonneville Salt Flats. It is the speedway where they do the speed trials for the world's fastest cars. It was awesome. I went 130mph with the salty wind swirling past me. My biggest mistake was thinking it was reasonable to let it out like that on the road. The cop said he was going 90 and losing me. If he had me on radar he probably would have had my bike towed. I wonder if the outcome would have been the same if another ethnicity had emerged from under my helmet. I might have been thrown in jail. But I did pay. That ticket cost me over $400. No regrets. I wrote a story about it for the local BMW motorcycle newsletter. I have a picture on the wall of my office of me riding on the salt flats.

My bride and I rode off on it on our wedding day, her white dress trailing behind, my green tie and cufflinks and black tux coordinated with the bike. It is an awesome picture. We once rode it to Victoria, BC and up into the Northern Cascades. I sold it the year before our eldest daughter was born. Our financial planner called it a threat to my "human capital," the brain and body that I was borrowing against in my pursuit of higher education. The e-bike is a lot safer. Its top speed is about 100mph less than my motorcycle's. We had a lot of adventures and still have the leathers and helmets in the closet. The motorcycle was a blast, but besides the danger aspect of it, it didn't offer a workout with the thrill.

The mid-drive e-bike is sweet. You have to pedal it or it won't go. The engineering involves a lot of torque and other engineering words I don't really understand. Basically it is magical to me. It is only a little bit cheating. It feels like having the wind at your back, which comes in handy when you're riding on the hilly streets of our city.

When I first rode one I was skeptical. I had been riding my Trek road bike a lot, prepping to ride from Seattle to Portland. 200+ miles with only my legs and lungs to power me. But my older brother was visiting from California and had an e-bike shop he wanted to check out. They offered test rides. I was curious. I tagged along and was soon facing a monster hill from the saddle of a shiny mid drive e-bike. I hit the pedals preparing to suffer, but the suffering never came. It was like I was riding on a flat road. My heart rate was up because I was pedaling, but I wasn't fighting to breathe. I was hooked.

I kept riding my road bike and completed the Seattle-to-Portland (STP) ride with my buddy. It was really hard, but so satisfying and something I still brag about to this day. It only took me about a week to recover. The big ride was over and I got complacent; nothing left to prove. I needed to work more exercise into my routine and my commute seemed to be my only downtime. I was putting on the weight that I had worked so hard to lose. Riding my regular bike downtown was a vigorous hilly trek that required a shower and changing in and out of spandex in my building locker room. It was great exercise, but over an hour all told. An e-bike could get me there in 40 minutes. No shower required. I bought the bike in December and promised my wife I would ride it year round. I bought all the best rain gear. Waterproof boots, pants, gloves, turtleneck/face mask fabric thing, and ear warmers. I used my old motorcycle gloves. I still had the leathers too, but those weren't so practical on a bicycle. The gloves had reinforced knuckles, in case of scraping along the ground or biker brawls.

This fall I stopped riding it in the rain, probably contributing to my depression, as I was getting very little exercise otherwise. I still haven't been riding it much, since I finished up at the day hospital, but I had a nice ride today. Picking up the Prozac was like grabbing a booster pack. It definitely gives me energy, helps to lift the fog. My bike's battery is lithium, like the pill I take at bedtime. I have an interesting relationship with lithium. I'd prefer to keep it connected to my bike in the garage than in my medicine cabinet. But for now, I am lithium-powered.

Being a white man is like riding an e-bike. Everyone else is on regular bikes. Sure, some of them are carbon fiber or have advanced gearing or other things, but they don't have the power. The raw structural power of generations of social engineering. Sure, you have to pedal on an e-bike to get where you're going, but you don't have to work as hard as those without the power, those experiencing systemic oppression. The gears of historical racism are powering me forward while others are pulled back.

But what about a white man that has a disability, especially an invisible one? How does intersectionality work there? In grad school the example often given was a woman of color who was a lesbian; she would have a different experience than a white woman who was a lesbian. That program was pretty focused on race and gender and sexuality, and didn't get much into the impact of disability. Certainly not white people with disabilities. I see plenty of white men stumbling around on the streets downtown gesturing to themselves. Black women too. Mental illness knows all colors. But in my case, when I recover, and I keep it secret, my white male privilege remains intact.

Occasionally I forget to charge up and run out of battery. Riding an e-bike with a dead battery is really difficult, but I always make it home. I struggle and sweat until I finally make it back to my battery charger. Those times when I run out of battery are when I'm most vulnerable. I fear that the next time I won't bounce back. Or my secret will get out and civilized society won't accept me back. But in my life I have the privilege to recharge, to take a break from work or school and not lose my health insurance or my housing or my paycheck. To recover. That is privilege. Sure, in some ways I've earned it, but those opportunities may have come easier to me because of who my grandfathers were.

I took off my bright green helmet and walked into the pharmacy to pick up my Prozac. No co-pay. I see my psychiatrist as much as I need to. I have good insurance. I have a good job. Men hired me for this job. Men who saw my ambition and my skills and my easy ability to blend right in with the team. I also worked my ass off for this opportunity. I am blessed and privileged. I have struggled too. But when my broken brain comes into balance I am free to step onto the field that was cleared by my confederate general great-great-grandfather and others that came before and after him. The challenge that I currently struggle with is, how do I promote equity while continuing to reach for success? I aspire for leadership roles, but we already have too many men who look like me in those roles. Am I taking the place of a more diverse group of candidates that haven't so easily risen toward these opportunities as I have?

How do I reconcile knowing that my privilege has buoyed my life, while giving credit that is due for the strength and accomplishment that is born from my struggle to survive and thrive with an invisible disability? I care about social justice. I treat everyone with respect. I watch for my own biases and microaggressions. I stumble. I have black friends, gay friends, female bosses, Asian colleagues. They all seem to like having me around. I make space for them. But I'm sure I fuck up and offend at times. But I am trying. I remain culturally curious and put high value on respect. I try to make amends when I'm made aware that I've offended someone. Parts of my life are diverse, others are very segregated. I spend most of my time with white people. I'm not sure how to reconcile this.

I heard at an equity training recently about the platinum rule, a step above the golden rule. Treat people not how you want to be treated, but how they want to be treated. That means paying attention and creating an awareness of the nuances of race and culture and ethnicity and gender. I would never claim to be "woke." That word annoys me. Anti-racism isn't a state you achieve. It is a stance. It is a commitment to equity, diversity, and inclusion, and a strong dose of humility.

In a country where I ride the e-bike of white male privilege, I can never shake off this birthright, however historically corrupt. But I can work for fairness and equity and not be colorblind or pretend that racism is a thing of the past. I know that not everyone has access to a psychiatrist with classical music in their lobby, especially if they don't look like me. I am working to change that. All of these promotions have put me in a position of influence. People listen to me. I am a behavioral health leader in one of the largest health systems in the United States. I have a responsibility to speak for those that don't have this voice. I know that recovery from mental illness is possible with the right treatment. I have lived it. No one deserves to suffer or die without access to care because of who their grandparents were. That is the equity I am fighting for in my work and in my life.

The drama of the gifted child

My daughter goes to a special school for gifted kids. It is called the highly capable cohort (HCC) program. She had to take tests and scored in the 99th percentile. Basically she is a smarty pants. With my background in disability services and mental health, I pretty quickly noticed that a number of the kids in her class have special needs. Autism, ADHD, anxiety, selective mutism, these are not uncommon diagnoses for kids that have high IQs. These kids are called "twice exceptional." They are very tuned in, very sensitive. Can you imagine having the intellectual acumen and reading ability of an adult, but the emotional experience of an 8-year-old? It has to be intense. Some of these kids are really anxious. Gifted and disabled. Exceling and struggling. Life is rarely straightforward. People are rarely uncomplicated.

Was I a gifted kid in a rural school who didn't know what to do with my kind of brain? Bookish and sensitive, I excelled in elementary school. I remember that they would send me to the library to read during English instruction and spelling tests because I was so far ahead of the other kids. By high school I struggled to keep my GPA above 3.5, probably due more to the apathy and depression than the academic challenge. I didn't really care, but my dad said I had to go to college. I think he saw that it was the only way out for a smart sensitive kid like me. I wouldn't do well in the world of uneducated men, was not good with my hands, not mechanical or particularly strong. I was kind of a wimp. The best thing I had going for me was my brain, but I didn't care.

I wonder what my experience would have been like if rather than sending me to the library where I was bored and falling behind what I was capable of, I was pushed to the limits of my potential and surrounded by peers that were able to keep up. I've noticed a similar sentiment with other parents of gifted kids; we don't want them to struggle the way we did. The agony and the ecstasy of an unrecognized high IQ. But many of us soldiered through, graduated from top-tier graduate schools and paid private school tuition from infancy through preschool—at least the cost of a college education, so that we could go to work and live out our potential. Juggling work and parenting and marriage and myself is the hardest challenge I have ever taken on. At least I'm not bored anymore.

I've had several rounds of neuropsychological testing. I was worried about my ongoing brain fog. I had a serious head injury, discharged from the hospital without concern, but I had a lingering worry that it has had a lasting effect. That, paired with medication that sometimes made my brain feel like it was running through molasses to process information, made me curious if it could be better. The testing provided sobering answers. It turns out that I did have significant processing delays, especially for my level of education and IQ. My IQ was high, in the superior range, but my memory and processing speed were in the bottom percentile. Reading and math are a challenge for me and my short-term memory is like Swiss cheese. I was also depressed, which didn't help matters either. The psychologist described my brain as "a Porsche with flat tires." Somehow though, despite my broken brain, I've managed to do all right. Since I dropped out of college I've never been unemployed, my income and prospects have steadily risen, I went to a top-ranked graduate school, and I work closely with doctors and engineers and MBAs, and I manage to keep up. However, many days I feel that I am barely keeping up. People seem to think I'm smart—a big vocabulary and sharp wit are great cover for executive functioning weaknesses that I try to keep just out of view.

I also wonder if my race and gender has anything to do with it. In my sociology studies and in candid conversations with women and people of color I have learned that white men are afforded a presumed competence. If I shave and put on nice clothes and walk in the room, it is assumed that I am smart and successful and have a lot to contribute. I assume it too, about myself. People have told me that I have a lot of confidence. They've never stepped inside my head.

Others have the opposite experience; other assumptions are made; they have a lot to prove. They internalize this negative bias. I have a lot to lose if I let my secret be known, not just that I am crazy, but that I am slow too. I sometimes worry about opening my mouth and being caught with a question that sends my flat tires spinning as I sputter to respond.

American Dreams

I continue to benefit from the inheritance of my grandfathers. I haven't seen a dime directly from their estates, but the indirect benefits of being a descendant of that generation of white men are immeasurable. They were the sons of immigrants, but they changed their names and blended into white society. ███████ and ███ changed easily to ███ and ███. They have been called the Greatest Generation: the generation that defeated Hitler, came back from WWII and participated in the longest, most prosperous time in American history. My grandfathers were awesome.

After the war, light-skinned men from any European country who had grown up here, had no accent, and had Americanized names, easily slipped past the discriminatory barriers that had held their parents back. The GI Bill sent them to college and then they went to work. The country prospered. America was booming. They had lots of babies. My Italian grandfather had 8 children. His boys succeeded in a white man's world: lawyers, executives, engineers. His only daughter became a doctor. This was the American Dream: that your children would do better than you. It still is the American Dream, however fleeting.

This was the experience of my family as we blended into the melting pot of white America. Immigrants who were from Asia or descendants of slaves couldn't just change their name and forget their accent to blend in. There is still a massive amount of white poverty in this country, exacerbated by generational factors, but if you can manage to slip past the gate, which usually involves a college degree, you have access to the privileges that generations of white men before you have carved out. The economists and sociologists have found that the average college-educated white man will most likely do better financially than a college-educated black woman. We have a long way to go.

My maternal grandparents, ████ and ████, marched with Dr. Martin Luther King, Jr. We recently watched the speech and read my grandfather's account in his memoir: a new MLK Day tradition. As I listened, I was saddened by how much of his dream was unrealized. The civil rights movement should not be part of history; it is a movement we should carry into our future.

These days I am focusing my efforts on creating equity in the mental health system, which has traditionally been poorly provisioned in communities of color. There is a lifetime of work to be done in this area. I struggle with how to balance the work to be done with my own desire to create an abundant and balanced life. I want to make a good living so that I can pay off my debt and buy a house and take vacations and send our kids to good schools. I am an American who has yet to give up on the dream. I want to help people and I want to be a good dad and take care of my family. I hope that it has a ripple effect. I put a lot of faith in the power of paying it forward.

I hope that my children will come visit me in my old age, and will make sure that their crazy old dad gets good care. Because all of us get old, experience disability, lose privilege. That loss of control is scary, especially for people with pre-existing conditions that they managed on their own for awhile. I want these little girls to be strong, smart women who can advocate for their parents, especially the one with the scary mental illness in his medical records.

Medicine Cabinet

I have a secret. I had a birthday party recently. We had over many of my friends (and all of their children). Many of them are colleagues from past jobs and continue to be an important part of my professional network. When cleaning the house my first stop was to the medicine cabinet. I've been to parties at other people's homes. I always look. The temptation is too great. I couldn't risk it.

I caught the shame in my eyes as I looked at my reflection in the mirrored cabinet. I opened it and faced the little orange bottles. I carried two fists full and buried them in my sock drawer. Lamictal, Cerzone, and Ambien were the current prescriptions I tucked away. For some reason I still had old bottles of Tegretol, lithium, and Seroquel, that I couldn't seem to part with. Those had to be hidden too. I left the prescription allergy and migraine medications. Somehow these were safe for public viewing. The other pill bottles though, they were not something I was ready to have other people aware of, even some of my closest friends. Even if unfamiliar, a quick Google search of these pills would let my secret out. I have a psychiatrist. I am being treated for a mood disorder. Google would quickly decode the esoteric names on the bottles into a list of potential diagnoses: insomnia, anxiety, depression, possibly bipolar disorder. These meds point to a defect in my mind, a big chink in the armor that I have built around me with a facade of normalcy. They point to a person who has grappled with serious mental illness and come out the other side. Unlike the survivors of cancer, those of us who survive serious mental health crises aren't likely to trumpet our success on social media and in our professional bios.

At various times in my life, since I began taking antidepressant medication at 19, I have tried to stop. I felt weak. Fists full of vitamins would be much more acceptable than one little pharmaceutical pill. In the culture I came from, taking these pills was the ultimate shame. If I only meditated more, bared more of my soul to another therapist, opened to the true bliss that was really me, ate more vegetables and less sugar, continued to rebel against our toxic mainstream society by standing for social justice, found my true passion, went back to school again, then I would be ok. Depression was a symptom of these imbalances, not a disease in itself. The science behind psychiatry was heavily criticized. In progressive circles we are raised to never question the science about climate change. Why, then, is it totally acceptable to question and ignore the science about mental illness?

I tried to quit, I really did. I ate right, I exercised, I went to therapy, I took lots of vitamins, but to no avail. The darkness always came back. One morning when I faced my executioner in the mirror once again, I wept and reached for the phone. I was sick, really sick, and I needed help.

I have come to terms, quietly, humbly, that for me, taking medication every day is what I need to do. If you read the message boards online, as I often have, people write about multiple medication trials, horrible side effects, unrelenting symptoms. Others encourage them to hang on and share that their doctor has finally found the right cocktail for them.

My doctor found mine. I take daily high doses of a mood stabilizer and antidepressant. My thoughts may be slightly dulled, my stomach slightly rounder, but otherwise I am no worse for wear. The darkness isn't allowed to get too close anymore. I have plenty of bad days, but I bounce back quicker. Some of this surely comes from experience and maturity, but a piece of it is chemical.

I am a little bit emotionally numb. I still laugh, I still cry, but I am a little flatter than I otherwise might be. This though, is nowhere near the flat shape that depression has hammered into me on so many occasions. It is much easier to laugh, to cry, to be present to my own life, when I am not ruminating on my failures and plotting my own demise. I am not weak. I am not broken. I have a disease. I have been treated with the best evidence-based pharmaceuticals and psychotherapies that modern medicine has to offer. I have great doctors.

I am normal. Typical. That is what I project to the world anyway. I have friends and colleagues who use wheelchairs or whose social graces reveal their autism or intellectual disability. They are "people with disabilities," a minority group that I am an ally of, but do not claim to be a member of. I have been impressed with one man, who is a self-advocate with cerebral palsy, who is not afraid to speak about his own experience with major depression. I keep my mouth shut; I am much safer hiding behind my privilege. I am stable now, confident that I won't be a hollering maniac on the street. I will never be shot or arrested for no good reason. I will always be able to find a good job. As long as I am stable anyway.

No one ever has to know about my disability, unless I tell them. Do I have one? On the first job application I applied for after college there was a page where you had to identify as having a disability or not. Major depression was listed as an example. At that time I was diagnosed with and taking medicine for that condition. I have completed this form many times and it always gives me pause.

I checked no. The last person I want to know about my troubles with emotional stability is a new employer. I come across as put together, intelligent, and capable. I am stable. I am white. I am a man in my late thirties. My resume reflects a steady, uninterrupted, rise in experience. I speak about marriage and fatherhood as a world I have been in for a long time and have no intention of abandoning. Dependable, responsible, trustworthy, solid. Depressed, anxious, scattered, suicidal. Those don't go together.

For now I will keep it to myself. Maybe someday I will stand in front of a room of strangers and tell my story. Maybe I will put my name on a book that lays my secrets out for the world. I'll go on "Ellen." But next time I have a party? I have no doubt that I'll empty my medicine cabinet into my sock drawer.

Stigma

Going to the doctor scares me. Not my psychiatrist, but the "regular" doctor for physical stuff. It turns out that crazy people get rashes and flus and headaches too. There it is in bold font at the top of my chart. **Bipolar Affective Disorder.** Every chart in the electronic health record has a snapshot section that starts with a problem list. I know this because I work in healthcare. It is the first thing a provider or their staff look at before they meet a new patient. It gives you a heads up for what you're walking into, because some visits can quickly become about more than just the "chief complaint," i.e. cough, headache, fever, anxiety, etc. You should be prepared so you're not blindsided. When I worked in primary care I overheard what the physicians and clinic staff sometimes said about patients with my diagnosis.

This is the only place where my secret isn't my own. I have been pretty open with select friends and family members about it, but that is often after knowing them for years and them knowing me before they knew my diagnosis. It is the other way around with providers; I suppose I made the appointment, but I didn't exactly choose to share my deepest secret with the dermatologist I saw for a one time consult for a weird looking mole on my back. My primary care doctor left his practice and I was afraid: he knew me, had seen me for years through ups and downs and knew I wasn't that crazy, the bad kind anyway, the kind that made his job harder. I had another doctor to manage that part of me. But he wrote about all the meds I was on and the diagnoses I had in his chart notes. Those weren't private conversations anymore. There was an electronic record of my crazy.

The morning of my intake appointment with the new primary care doctor, I carefully picked out a professional outfit, Northwest dress casual: a pressed shirt and khaki pants and brown leather shoes in need of a polish. I wore my employee badge from a lanyard prominently hanging from my neck. It had my picture and my credentials on it. That guy on the badge: he's got his shit together and isn't going to cause any trouble. I had rehearsed my story about my job in my cubicle in the skyscraper across the street. The new doctor was perfectly nice. He brought up my high cholesterol and encouraged me to get more exercise, affirmed that I was generally healthy but could always do better: regular well visit stuff. It was a short visit but he did a good job of not making it feel rushed.

But he didn't ask me about my other health condition. I waited and waited and he never did. The medical assistant had verified my prescriptions and I know the doctor reviewed them. But he never said a word about them. I was relieved it was over. In later visits we talked about migraines and allergies but never my other diagnosis. But I think by now I've convinced him I'm not the bad kind of crazy. I no longer wear my badge to the clinic and sometimes even wear a hat and jeans and don't bother to shave.

Last year I went to the emergency department for a migraine that wouldn't stop. After waiting for an eternity of agony I was checked in and hooked up to a cocktail of Benadryl and magnesium and anti-nausea medication and fluids. I covered my eyes from the bright light until I fell asleep in the oversized chair behind a curtain in the busy ER. Doctors and nurses came and went. My wife texted that she and my daughters were in the lobby. My brother and his wife came. I was pretty out of it. I started to come to and a nurse woke me up and asked me if I was ready to leave. She seemed impatient, colder than the nurse that had so gently connected my IV. I was groggy and unsure, still in some pain. I asked to see the doctor. She sighed and walked out of the room silently. The doctor came and prescribed more medicine. No opiates or painkillers or anything like that. I just wanted some relief. I fell back asleep and the next time I awoke I was more alert. The nurse came and asked me if I could stand. I offered to try. I slowly rose, towering above her; she looked nervous, and quickly said "I think you're fine now... I'll go tell the doctor you're ready to go now." In my vulnerable state I was put off by her abruptness, her seeming minimization of my pain, and what I read into as some skepticism of my need to be there at all.

"Malingering" is a word I learned early in my career. It is when someone comes to the doctor or hospital and pretends to have an illness so that they can get time off from work or drugs that they don't really need. My fear, which I'm sure is based more in stigma than in fact, is that people will see my diagnosis and assume I also have a drug problem (which I never have) or have a tendency to exaggerate symptoms because I am crazy or just plain lazy. Or maybe a mental illness does or doesn't even exist and all of this is true about me.

Now, in defense of healthcare providers, as I am one, this does happen with some patients, and their diagnostic history is a clue that it might, but you have to be careful to not let that bias creep in. Subtle, even fleeting unconscious judgements affect how we treat and interact with people.

Later, when my headache was gone and my faculties came back, I thought about that nurse. It was subtle but I felt it. Was she just having a bad day, was the ER over capacity and she needed to free up the bed, or did she see my diagnosis in the chart and sense that I might be a problem and she should treat me as such? Maybe all of the above? I'll never know... but now I have some appreciation for what my black friends experience when someone is disrespectful, though their experiences are magnified, I am sure.

It's little moments like these that keep me in the closet, and make me want to make sure this secret stays buried from any-one that doesn't have enough time to get to know me enough to understand my story. To know that the words on the screen are only a small part of who I am.

Am I crazy to publish this book? It seemed like a great idea when I started. Share my secrets with the world. No more shame. Stigma be damned. This is how we bust stigma, right? The guy next door, or in the office, with the minivan and the cute kids and the pretty wife and the good job has a serious mental illness. Just a regular person like you. But as I work through drafts of this book, I consider using a pseudonym. John Smith sounds like a good one at the moment. I could change a few details. Anyone that knows me well could figure it out, but the rest of the world, the internet, would be left wondering who the real John Smith was. If anyone cared at all. I would lose my job and my license if I shared the PHI, or personal health information, of any patient the way I have shared my own in this book. Will I lose my job if I share this? Will people congratulate my bravery and then eye me with concern and suspicion forever after?

I haven't decided what to do, but I want to share the truth of who I am, of what I have been through, whether it is under my name or a made-up one. Maybe there is another way. Where did I put that Sharpie?

14

Wounded Healer

Over the past 100 years the field of mental health, particularly psychiatry, has vacillated between a psychodynamic and a
biological perspective on the causes of mental illness. And by
determining and labeling the cause, the practitioner bases their
treatment on this diagnosis. Psychodynamic, psychoanalytic
thought (think Freud, Jung) focuses on how the experiences of
childhood, often trauma and/or mistreatment in childhood by

parental figures, can lead to mental illness in adulthood. The roots of this trauma must be explored, talked about, unconscious drives brought conscious, with the hope of emotional catharsis and insight leading to healing. Biological psychiatry, on the other hand, focuses on genetic and brain-based factors —separating the context, the environment, from the illness. This approach came about in the age of psychopharmacology. A group of psychiatrists witnessed relatively fast recovery by treating people with medications that would have taken years to treat with psychoanalysis. My theory is that the ones that weren't very good at psychoanalysis, maybe didn't have the people skills necessary, but were very good scientists, found biological psychiatry much more in line with the laboratory roots of their mainstream medical education. They were crappy therapists but brilliant psycho-pharmacologists. The debate rages on as to what is the most effective treatment; there are hundreds of psychotherapies and medications to try, some of which have a strong evidence base for treating certain conditions. A combination of approaches is often most effective; medication and psychotherapy, depending on the severity and type of condition.

I've been a therapist now, a legit independently-licensed therapist, for over five years. But I've been a "clinician" for over 10. People have been legitimately calling me their therapist, counselor, social worker, or case manager since then. Those 10 years included grad school practicums (internships) and several years of post-graduate practice under the supervision of an independently-licensed therapist. But the funny thing about all this "supervision" is that you are really doing all of this on your own; they aren't in the room with you while you're pretending, fumbling to be of help. Once a week you sit with your supervisor and discuss cases. I have heard of supervisors that watch videos of their supervisees, but in my case it has always been my self-report that they listen to.

I've been working in clinical roles for over ten years. I've been doing this for a long time. They say it takes 10 years to become a really skilled therapist. Malcolm Gladwell has a 10,000 hour theory about the length of time it takes to master anything. Steven Hayes, in response to Gladwell, says you can do something badly for 10,000 hours and not get any better if you are doing it incorrectly or without a growth (vs fixed) mindset. I have to agree with Hayes. I am 10,000 hours in at this point, but they call it having a practice for a reason.

Wounded Healer

I recently renewed an interest in Jungian archetypes in the most unlikely of places: YouTube. I was reviewing a clip on Joseph Campbell's hero's journey, as I tried to breathe new life into a decades-old screenplay I had just dusted off. Amazingly, revisiting this hobby I once considered for a career led me right back to my current vocation as a psychotherapist. YouTube suggested a related clip that caught my eye; a psychoanalyst giving a talk on Chiron, The Wounded Healer. I have often heard of the concept of the wounded healer; those who enter this work, in part to try and save their own soul by helping others, and thrive in it because of their ability to empathize with those struggling with the psychic pain that they too have danced with.

I had not heard, however, of this fellow named Chiron, the centaur whose myth forms the archetype for a medicine man cursed with eternal pain who dedicates his life to helping others with theirs. As the story goes, this teacher and physician, blessed with immortality, was pierced by a poison spear. He couldn't die, but instead was forever wracked with the pain of burning poison in his veins. Eventually, Hercules made a deal with Zeus to save the life of cursed Prometheus. Chiron took up his chains and was allowed to die, picked apart by eagles until he was no more.

Wow, what a story! It helps me to make meaning of my own journey. A teacher once pointed out to me that many going into this field do so searching for a cure to their own struggle and/or that of their family. This is not the place to find it. They should put an auto-reply on graduate school program applications warning would-be therapists that a cure to what ails them won't be bestowed upon graduation or licensure.

Research indicates that large numbers of mental health professionals have experienced mental health problems of their own. I certainly have my own share of issues. In my experience, the profession doesn't heal us, but it transforms us into healers. Those dark nights of our souls are transmuted into calm reassurance and wise words for our clients in the sacred moments they share their raw emotional pain with us.

Once I dreamed of making movies and telling stories; now I collect them and do my best to influence their bearers toward a better place.

I'd do anything to heal the raw Chironic wound that sometimes grips my soul, but until the gods grant me relief, I will be down here serving those who call out for the presence of one who isn't afraid of sitting in the dark with them. I'm still holding out hope that if I join them on their road to salvation, I might just stumble upon my own.

15

Order of Operations

My writing was just interrupted by a friendly visitor. I was really in the zone and felt the pull to keep going. But I pause, close the laptop and look up. My 2-year-old is standing there, in her little blue dress, holding a partially deflated purple ball. With eyes wide as the ocean and a smile brighter than the sun, she says, "Daddy, will you play ball with me?" with sweet sincerity. She is irresistible. When I lost the will to live, I lived for her. This angel deserves a Daddy. I am tempted to open the laptop and tell her I am working, but I feel a muscle flex in my heart and a warmth in my throat. "Of course." I put the laptop aside and she tosses me the ball. She laughs out loud. "Daddy, you caught the BALL! Now throw it to me." She is already in charge, and I am at her service.

This moment with her reminds me of another kid that wanted to play ball during my graduate school internship at a middle school. "What do you want to be when you grow up?" I heard the middle school teacher ask the kid who was not even a teenager yet. "You're going to college, right?" This was said almost as a statement, a demand, rather than a question. In this poor urban middle school, college is pushed on these kids as the only way out of the poverty of their upbringing. If they fail to achieve the outcome that a career beyond college promises, they will just be another cautionary tale, another case of potential squandered by someone who may have just been unworthy in the first place. It strikes me that this approach, laced with undertones of fear, shame, and guilt, may be causing more harm than good. As these kids grow up, the weight of these heavy expectations may prove to be too much at times, a burden that they may seek to ease with drugs, alcohol, sex, or the only acceptable path: achievement. Achievement was my path, and it turned into an addiction.

The problem is, for those that do make it, who survive the grueling marathon that is college and career, some struggle to let go of the burden of those expectations. What is left to do once you've achieved what you were told to do, when you have refrained from the excesses of your less successful peers, and now your resume and Facebook and LinkedIn page sparkles with success? Something may be missing, something lost along the way, a journey so focused on the future that one has lost the ability to be present and enjoy the fruits of your hard-won life.

When you wake up wondering what the point of it all is, it is time to chart a new course: this time with the goal of being wide awake to the present moment, with an eye on the future, but your full self in the now. It is time to escape the tunnel vision that has thus far defined your path. "So, any idea about what you want to do someday?" I asked the kid with a wink. "I don't know," he shrugged, "can we go play ball now?" I smiled, grateful for this invitation to step back into the moment. The future can be a pretty daunting place to live, but right now in this moment, it's time to play ball.

The irreverent toddler cackles and throws the ball at my head, so pleased to be in this moment with me. Once again I pull from my reverie on the past. I cackle too and bat the ball back to her.

My mind continues in the background, thinking of ideas for the intro to this book. But my eyes and my arms and my legs and my heart are here with my baby girl. I am learning to let my mind go on in the background while I do what is most meaningful, most important. This rambunctious toddler is the greatest mindfulness teacher I have ever had. She lives in the moment. She embodies mindfulness all the time. It isn't something to practice, a state to try to get back to, a discipline to be mastered. It comes naturally. I hope she never loses this ability, but I already see my 8-year-old caught in the past and future.

But when we play we are all right there. "Sister, sister, come throw the ball with us." There we are, standing in the living room on Saturday morning in our pajamas. A simple moment of family life. Of connection. I love these girls to the moon and back. This latest experience of recovery has grounded me. It has put in perspective what is important, what is priority.

A therapist once reminded me that life and relationships should be prioritized in the following order. 1. Self. 2. Spouse. 3. Children. 4. Work. I nodded my head and figured that was important, but impossible. I would have pretended that was my priority, but before I went to the day hospital, before I once again seriously considered ending my life, that was certainly not the order of operations of my life. 1. Work. 2. Children. 3. Spouse. 4. Self was more accurate.

It isn't anymore. I hold work more lightly, no longer excusing myself from engaging with my children because I had work to do to pay for their expensive life, their expensive future. That approach exhausted me. I missed the fact that they power me. They give my life purpose. Their energy is infectious. The girls soon move on... the ball rolls to a stop across the room. I hear them talking in the other room about an art project. I go back to my writing. I have more energy. I write about this moment.

I am a father. This home has a father in it. My fathers and grandfathers are all gone, but they left me with a legacy of what it is to be a good man. I learned as much or more from their failures as I did from their successes. They weren't around very much. I am staying so that my children see me every morning instead of every other weekend. I pay a lot of child support, not court ordered, but because I am here, every day, raising these beautiful children with my lovely wife.

This is commitment, this is love, this is family. I am blessed and still learning to accept that I am worthy of so much love. Worthy of being an integral part of this amazing little family of ours. I am blessed.

16

Acceptance and Commitment

I'm getting fat again. 10 pounds turned into 20 turned into 30 turned into 50. I am nearly 250 lbs. The numbers are going up. I bought new pants. I got rid of all of my 38" waisted pants the last time I got in shape. A few months ago I ordered more, stashing my 36" pants in the back of my closet. Today when I got dressed I thought maybe I should swallow shame and order some 40" slacks. Comfort over vanity.

I'm eating a lot of sugar. I'm totally addicted to peanut butter cups and chocolate covered almonds and salami. When I'm in this place of overcarbinating, it isn't that I don't care about my health or how I look. I think about it a lot. But I am also tired and need an easy pick me up, chocolate eases my sadness and my lethargy, despite causing more on the back end. This cycle is not new. I have no doubt I'll get a fire under me again, quit the carbs and cycle the fat away. But when? I am going to the doctor for my annual physical soon. I have no doubt that my cholesterol is sky high again and that my glucose is trending in the direction of prediabetes. I'm almost 40. How many more cycles of this do I get before a heart attack or stroke or diabetes are part of the story?

My friends and I have been talking about riding our bikes to Canada at the end of the summer. The last time I committed to a 200 mile ride I lost 40 pounds - I improved my diet, I did inter-mittent fasting every day, I cut way back on sugar, I was disci-plined. I exercised almost every day. I looked good. I felt good. I got a new wardrobe. People applauded my effort to get healthy. It wasn't the first time I had been a fitness success story, and at the rate I am going, it won't be the last.

My weight has been a rollercoaster my whole adult life. I weighed about 175 when I finished high school, 190 when I met my wife, 240 when I got married, 215 the first time I rode my bike 100 miles in a day, and 248 today. I am estimating because I don't have the courage to face the scale at this moment. I'm an overall large guy, so I manage to carry it, but I'd rather be long and lean than big and tall. Medication has certainly affected my metabolic health. I imagine that if medication weren't part of my journey, my weight may have fluctuated 20 lbs up and down, but certainly not 75 lbs.

I do not want to accept being fat, being overweight, but I have to if anything is going to change. I won't fit into those 36" pants until I admit that I can't fit into them and I get rid of them. That has been my experience in the past. In tandem with my weight gain and loss journey has been my journey with my bipolar disorder. I used to think of my health, both physical and mental, as linear with an end state of good health: a healthy mind and body. I know now that that will not be my journey, past or future. My weight and my moods will fluctuate for the rest of my life. My stability depends on medications that affect my metabolism. I hate it, but I am accepting it. I also can choose to eat healthier, to exercise, and to better manage my stress. A health crisis can come at any time; cancer, accidents, so many things can injure our fragile bodies and minds that we have no control over. But even so, we can choose to be healthy within the context of our situation. For me that is a morning smoothie, meat and vegetables, avoiding alcohol and sweets and chips, getting 8 hours of sleep, riding my bike a few times a week, daily mindfulness and time in nature. Bad stuff still happens, my mood still goes up and down, but when I do these things, life just goes a little bit smoother, I am a little more resilient and able to more gracefully address whatever the day presents.

I am a teacher and practitioner of an approach called Acceptance and Commitment Therapy, or ACT. (It's said as the word "act", rather than separate letters, as in A.C.T.) Over the last year I have felt like I went through the looking glass and am just now making sense of what happened. Not much has changed, yet everything has changed. I still work too much, my relationships are stressful, I'm out of shape, and I take a lot of medication. But something is distinctly different. The fear of losing my mind is lessened. I lost it and I took a break and I came back. I'm getting that promotion after all. I'm ok. If I hadn't taken a break I probably wouldn't be.

The main tenet of ACT is that life is hard and will always be hard. Bad things happen. The full range of human experiences and emotions is inherently painful. Life is full of ups and downs. No one can escape it. We all die, and everyone we love will die too. ACT asserts that a fair amount of human difficulty arises when we resist this reality. Our finely-honed problem-solving brains, adept at building houses and highways and creating art, are not able to solve the problem of our own emotions. Our capitalist society provides no end of solutions for our pain, some of them well-meaning. Our current opioid crisis is the most glaring example, but we can overindulge in anything with the goal of neutralizing pain. ACT asserts that to live life to the fullest, one must embrace the pain and learn skills to navigate more successfully through it. This high level of resilience is called psychological flexibility. The goal is to be more present in your day-to-day life and take committed actions that lead to living out your values. Noticing when you're hooked and distracted by battling pain, and unhooking from that, is essential. Pain + resistance = suffering. Pain + acceptance = pain that is easier to move through gracefully. What I am struggling with lately is, with my diagnosis of bipolar disorder: what are emotions to be accepted, versus symptoms to address with medication? I like the concept of workability—does an action lead toward a fuller life or a smaller one? In my case medication is not an avoidance of pain, but an acceptance of my mood disorder. Knowing the history of my biological father's undiagnosed and untreated manic depressive mind helps me to accept this as my fate. It helps me to feel less guilty. I have lately been referring to bipolar disorder as something I inherited. It helps with the shame that if only I was stronger I could overcome the symptoms on my own and wouldn't have to see a psychiatrist or have to take medicine every day.

This is my life. It is full of contradiction and grace. I am lucky to be alive. I will be down again and will go back up, maybe too far up. I am learning to ride the waves. I know what works and what doesn't. I have good people to hold tight to when the waves overcome me. I'm looking forward to tomorrow.

This is not **the end**.
It is only the beginning.

About the Author

██ ████ is a psychotherapist in private practice and a behavioral health leader in a large healthcare organization. He is a passionate advocate for improving access to high-quality mental health care. He is a sought-after speaker on the topics of professional wellness and burnout, acceptance and commitment therapy, and telehealth. He has a Bachelor of Arts ████████████████████ College and a Master of ████████ from the University ████████. He is a Licensed ████████ ████████ in five states. In his spare time he reads crime novels, pushes his kids on the swings, goes grocery shopping, cooks without using recipes, and rides his bike in the rain. He lives in the Pacific Northwest with his wife and two daughters. He is surrounded by unicorns. This is his first book.

Acknowledgements

Special thanks go to my brother-in-law ███, without whom all of this would flow a lot less clearly; to ███, my copy editor for life; and to my publisher ███ for believing in this project and bringing it to the page. I also want to thank the dear family, friends, colleagues, and professionals who I felt safe enough to share some of these stories with before I ever wrote them down. The gratitude I have would fill volumes. Thank you.